BEHIND THE HEADLINES
American History's Schemes, Scandals and Escapades

BEHIND THE HEADLINES

American History's Schemes, Scandals and Escapades

Webb Garrison

Stackpole Books

Copyright © 1983 by Webb Garrison

Published by
STACKPOLE BOOKS
Cameron and Kelker Streets
P.O. Box 1831
Harrisburg, PA 17105

All rights reserved, including the right to reproduce this book or portions thereof in any form or by any means, electronic or mechanical, including photocopying, recording, or by any information storage and retrieval system, without permission in writing from the publisher. All inquiries should be addressed to Stackpole Books, Cameron and Kelker Streets, P.O. Box 1831, Harrisburg, Pennsylvania 17105.

Printed in the U.S.A.

Library of Congress Cataloging in Publication Data

Garrison, Webb B.
  Behind the headlines.

  Includes index.
  1. United States—History—Miscellanea.
2. Corruption (in politics)—United States—History—Miscellanea. I. Title.
E179.G24 1983   973   83-469
ISBN 0-8117-0817-9

Contents

Introduction	9
Washington, D.C. – How the Site Was Chosen for the Nation's Capital	11
William Franklin, Benjamin's Tory Son	16
When Frederick, Maryland Paid Ransom to the Confederates	21
Rutherford B. Hayes – Stolen Votes Elected Loser to White House	25
John Tyler – How He Seized the White House as Vice President	30
The Marshall Decision – Source of the Supreme Court's Power	34
Luck – The Big Factor in the Battle of Antietam	38
British Boundary Dispute Spawned Mason/Dixon Line	42
Currier & Ives – A Thriving Business Built on Calamities	45
Grover Cleveland – The Presidential Candidate Who Overcame Scandal	49
George Selden – The Man Who Patented the Automobile	53

The Regicides—They Escaped Death through Shelter by the Puritans	58
Nathaniel Palmer—Youthful Discoverer of Antarctica	62
Drug Addiction through Civil War Medication	65
John Sutter—How the Gold Rush Wiped Out His Fortune	68
Orville Wright and "Plane Fever"	72
Britain's American Colony Snatched by Spain	76
The Scheme to Pay Thomas Jefferson's Debts through a Lottery	80
Mary Walker, M.D.—First Female Medic Won Congressional Medal of Honor	84
How a Riverboat Quarrel Saved Mark Twain's Life	89
Confederate Warship Fought Civil War Long After Lee's Surrender	94
Daniel Butterfield and the Bugle Call "Taps"	98
Martin Van Buren Defeated by $3,665	101
The Edison/Westinghouse "War of Currents"	105
Aaron Burr—The Fugitive Who Presided Over the Senate	109
Samuel Langley—Who Should Have Been the First to Fly a Plane	112
Sequoyah's Printing Press Threatened White Man	117

How President Tyler's Life was Saved by a Song	120
"Uncle Tom's Cabin" — Dramatized against Its Author's Wishes	123
Influential British Sympathetic to American Revolution	130
Pullman Cars — First Put on Tracks for Lincoln's Funeral	136
Booker T. Washington — Diplomat or Uncle Tom	141
Detective William Burns — Crude Bombs Propelled Him to Fame	146
Leland Stanford's Love of Horses Helped Develop Movies	151
High Jinks on Capitol Hill	155
Eleven Days that Disappeared in 1752	160
John Wesley and His Romance that Started the Methodist Church	164
Emancipation Proclamation Was Psychological Warfare	168
Thomas Nast's Pen Toppled an Empire	173
John Paul Jones Took a Revolution to Britain	178
William Paterson — New Jersey's Delegate Triggered Development of the U.S. Senate	183
Congress Took 34½ Years to Sanction Standard Time	187
Index	190

Introduction

Most of the persons and events described in this book are widely familiar. Many of the names used here are household words.

Yet I dare to hope that few if any of the graphic details provided in this collection are universally known. Not simply newspaper journalists, but history book authors as well, face problems of selection. Space is limited. Not everything can be included; something must be omitted.

Frequently a vital link in a chain of events, or an unexpected set of contributing factors helping to shape what we call greatness, is missing from standard treatments of noted persons and history-making events.

It is the purpose of this volume to provide a few such vital links and sets of contributing factors. Though the goal of spreading information in readable fashion is basic, I do dare to hope that every vignette here will prove interesting—even entertaining.

Style somewhat like that normally used for newspaper feature articles has been employed, again for the sake of readability. Each vignette is the product of meticulous research; all facts can be verified —though not always in readily accessible sources.

Grateful acknowledgement is made for encouragement received from readers and staff members of media in which some of the subjects here were earlier treated in different fashion: The Atlanta *Journal-Constitution,* The *National Enquirer,* and The Evansville (Indiana) *Press.* Surprisingly—in the light of lurid headlines and sensational stories about celebrities—the *National Enquirer* demands total documentation of every historical article published. No other publication in the world is more exacting at this point.

Here's hoping you'll *enjoy* learning from these vignettes.

WEBB GARRISON

"Washington City" remained a sleepy river village long after it was designated as the new site of the U.S. government

Political "Log Rolling" Placed the Permanent Capital of the U.S. on Then-Desolate Banks of the Potomac River

Noted French designer and builder Pierre Charles L'Enfant won lasting fame as the architect who laid out Washington, D.C. But it was the doggedness and political acumen of one American—Alexander Hamilton—that led to the selection of the site on which L'Enfant planned "the ideal city."

Movements of British troops plus sectional rivalry had caused the Continental Congress to shift the site of its sessions from one place to another. First Philadelphia, then Baltimore. Back to Philadelphia and on to York and to Lancaster, Pennsylvania, before returning to Philadelphia. On to Princeton, Annapolis, Trenton and finally, New York City.

Changes in the seat of government made it awkward and sometimes impossible for legislators to take along records and files. Travel was often so difficult that attendance was low; meeting in Nassau Hall (a college building) at Princeton, business was conducted by just twenty-two members. Long before independence became assured, there was an attempt to establish a permanent seat of government. The November, 1779, suggestion that first entered official records favored purchase of "a few square miles near Princeton village, whereon to erect public offices and buildings."

If city fathers of Kingston, New York, knew of the sentiment favoring Princeton, they looked at it askance. Early in 1783 they asked the state legislature to put its weight behind their proposal to grant Congress one square mile within the limits of the town of Kingston as "a separate district for the Honorable Congress of the United States." Alexander Hamilton, who later became the most influential figure in the fight for location of the capital, persuaded New Yorkers to increase the Kingston offer to two square miles.

Nothing came of the proposal, though. Neither was there any action upon an offer from Annapolis in May of the same year. In June, New Jersey offered to provide a site anywhere in the colony. Virginia countered by proposing to give up the town of Williamsburg plus 300 acres of land and cash not exceeding £100,000.

Then meeting in Philadelphia, Congress proposed to take up the various offers in October. Long before that date rolled around, mutinous unpaid Revolutionary soldiers forced lawmakers to flee from Independence Hall. They adjourned hastily with plans to meet eight days later in Princeton; some vowed never again to convene in the City of Brotherly Love. A committee headed by James Madison solemnly considered the matter of a permanent seat of government and submitted a formal report on September 18, 1783.

No action was taken by Congress, but one aspect of the Madison report quickly gained informal but lasting concensus. The permanent site of national government would be a "federal district" under direct control of Congress and not included in the boundaries of any state. Such a concept, which required a radical break with European tradition, was not absolutely novel. Centuries earlier, aware of intense

"Washington City" as it appeared in 1800
—Library of Congress

rivalry between Israel and Judah, King David had established Jerusalem as just such a federal capital.

It would take more than the wisdom of David, though, to persuade rival delegations to yield their claims for the prize. Briefly, lawmakers seriously considered having not one but two capitals. Francis Hopkinson ridiculed that proposal by suggesting that a recently-authorized statue of George Washington should be "placed on wheels and be taken to the site of the nation's business, wherever that might be."

Adoption of the Constitution in 1787 settled for all time the question of jurisdiction—which was given to Congress in keeping with prevailing sentiment. But the matter of location remained a wide-open and hotly-debated issue. New York, the site of government at the time our first president was inaugurated, naturally wanted to remain the political as well as financial center of the nation. A southern bloc led by James Madison and Richard Lee argued persuasively for a capital on the banks of the Potomac River—"geographically, the center of the United States."

George Washington made no secret of the fact that he'd like very much to see the government centered near his beloved Mount Vernon.

But even his enormous prestige was not enough to sway northern votes. Lawmakers were in a hopeless deadlock with the line of division being geographical: north versus south.

Congress had shown itself impotent to act upon another issue that many considered far more pressing. Debts incurred by the several colonies that later became independent states were staggering. Secretary of the Treasury Alexander Hamilton had drafted and presented an Assumption Bill under which the new nation would assume the debts of its member states. No other course seemed remotely likely to restore credit and bring economic stability. But war debts of northern states were generally much greater than those of southern. Many southern delegates balked at helping to foot bills run up by northerners. Hamilton was a few votes short of having the number required to pass his Assumption Bill—and there was no indication that its foes would yield.

In this critical situation, Thomas Jefferson returned from France to become Washington's Secretary of State. According to Jefferson's own decidedly lame explanations years afterward, his four-year absence made him ignorant of internal dissension so great that some members of Congress were beginning to talk of withdrawing from the new union.

Hamilton was a veteran practitioner of the subtle art of political vote-trading, or "log rolling." He saw his opportunity and rose to the occasion superbly. In a private meeting with Jefferson, he proposed that if the Secretary of State would persuade a few southerners to vote for the Assumption Bill, the Secretary of the Treasury—properly grateful—would persuade a few northerners to throw their weight behind the proposal to locate the permanent capital of the U.S. in the south.

Precisely how many votes were traded is a matter of conjecture; clearly, it was not more than a handful. But a switch of one or two senators and perhaps half a dozen representatives was enough. Congress voted to have the U.S. assume war debts of the states—and to locate the federal capital on the banks of the Potomac (where George Washington wanted it).

A July 16, 1790, bill established Philadelphia as the site of Congress until the first Monday in December, 1800. Then the government would move to a Potomac River site. George Washington himself negotiated terms under which on March 30, 1791, nineteen landed proprietors ceded their rights—some reluctantly—to about 600 acres needed to supplement land given by Virginia.

Even when the official transfer of power from Philadelphia to the new federal city was made in 1800, Washington was "a mud hole in the middle of a forest." Congressman John C. Smith of Connecticut described Pennsylvania Avenue as "a deep morass covered with elder bushes." Northern newspapers dubbed it "the Serbonian Bog." Portugal's minister to the U.S., the witty Abbe Correa de Serra, took a look at the new capital and dubbed it "the city of magnificent distances."

Senator Gouverneur Morris, in a private letter, confessed that "We only need here houses, cellars, kitchens, scholarly men, amiable women, and a few other such trifles to possess a perfect city, for we can walk over it as we would in the fields and woods, and, on account of a strong frost, the air is quite pure." Abigail Adams, on her way to the new "presidential palace" that was far from finished, lost her way in the woods and with her party wandered for two hours before being rescued.

From the steps of the Capitol, according to contemporary accounts, a person could count "seven or eight boarding-houses, one tailor's shop, one shoemaker's, one printing establishment, the home of a washwoman, a dry-goods house and an oyster market." It was from that beginning—determined not by national sentiment but by political vote-trading—that present-day Washington, D.C., rose from the wilderness.

Governor William Franklin, staunchly Tory son of Benjamin

Benjamin Franklin's Son, Disowned after a Quarrel over Politics, Never Effected a Reconciliation with His Father

William Franklin (1731-1813) was the last British governor of New Jersey. He was the "natural" (illegitimate) son of Benjamin Franklin and until middle life was the apple of his father's eye. During the American Revolution, William turned against democracy and his father. He remained a staunch Tory so was disowned by Benjamin; later attempts at reconciliation were unsuccessful.

Much evidence supports the view that William was the son of Benjamin's common-law wife, Deborah Read. But there is no documentary evidence. Though most Americans vaguely remember that

Ben Franklin's son was involved in his famous kite experiment, few pause to wonder how he got there—or what became of him. Silence of history books may be due to respect for the memory of one of America's most gifted leaders.

Benjamin Franklin's son grew up in Philadelphia, where he showed "great fondness for books." Later he entered military service and acquitted himself so well that he became a captain in the Pennsylvania forces at eighteen. A year later his famous father wrote of him: "William is now nineteen years of age, a tall proper Youth, and much of a Beau. He acquired a habit of idleness in the military expedition, but begins of late to apply himself to business. I hope he will become an industrious man."

It was Billy who got his father's kite into the air in 1752 when the latter showed electricity to be "the vital force in lightning." But instead of the boy of twelve or fifteen who is universally depicted in that incident, Billy was actually a military veteran aged twenty-one. For his role in the investigation of lightning, Billy won the M.A. degree from Oxford University.

Benjamin Franklin started writing his famous *Autobiography* for his son—partly because of gratitude for Billy's role in helping to draw electricity from the sky.

Through his father's influence young William served for a period as clerk of the house of the Assembly of Pennsylvania. Then Benjamin got him an appointment as comptroller of the general postoffice—a job he held from 1754 to 1756. When his father went to England in 1756 as agent for Pennsylvania, William resigned from his post and went with him.

In England young Franklin studied law and was admitted to the bar. William Strahan, a close friend of his father, described William as "one of the prettiest young gentlemen I ever knew from America. His father is at one and the same time his friend, his brother, his intimate and easy companion."

Both of the Franklins became close friends of Scottish-born John Stuart, Earl of Bute. Bute was a lord of the bedchamber to the Prince of Wales, so had great influence when the prince became King George III in 1760. Almost as soon as George III ascended the throne he began getting recommendations from Bute that William Franklin be appointed to a high post in the colonies.

After secret negotiations, in August, 1762, the monarch named

Benjamin Franklin's son as royal governor of New Jersey. "Know you that we reposing especial trust and confidence in the prudence courage and loyalty of you, the said William Franklin, have thought fit to constitute and appoint you to be our Captain General and Governor in Chief in and over our provinces of Nova Caesarea or New Jersey," the royal commission read in part.

With his father as an onlooker, William placed his hand upon a Bible and swore to obey and uphold the authority of King George III in New Jersey. Governor Franklin reached that colony from England on February 23, 1763. He was well received and showed himself to be an able administrator.

But tensions that had been mounting between Britain and her American colonies for a decade reached a crisis point in 1774. On February 2 of that year the elder Franklin wrote his son to urge: "I wish you were well settled on your farm. 'Tis an honester and a more honourable because a more independent employment."

Later that year, father and son met at Perth Amboy and had a long talk about the conflict that both saw as inevitable. Benjamin urged American resistance at any cost; his son disagreed and insisted that his loyalties were totally committed to the English crown.

Benjamin Franklin sadly chose to put loyalty to his country above love for his son. Brief notes that he made when the First Continental Congress assembled indicate that he recognized himself to be "perhaps the loneliest man in the crowded chamber of the Pennsylvania State House." That loneliness stemmed from the fact that at a distance of only half a day's journey, Governor Franklin was persuading members of the New Jersey Assembly to "avoid exposing this fair land to the royal heel."

The break between father and son was complete. Benjamin was wholly committed to armed rebellion; William was equally dedicated to England and the king. So Governor Franklin remained at his post after armed conflict broke out, and continued to collect and transmit intelligence to England.

On June 15, 1776, the Provincial Congress of New Jersey declared Benjamin Franklin's son to be "an enemy to the liberties of this country," and ordered his arrest. He was sent as a prisoner to Connecticut, and for a time was quartered at East Windsor. In 1778 he was exchanged and released, so went to New York for a four-year stay during which he served for a time as President of the Board of Associated Loyalists (or Tories).

Benjamin Franklin with grandsons on streets of Paris (from watercolor by Henry A Ogden)

The son of America's great diplomat, scientist, and philosopher left his homeland in 1782 and never came back. As compensation for the losses he had sustained the English government granted him a cash settlement of £1,800 plus a pension of £800 per year for life.

Ten years after he had quarreled with his father over politics William tried to effect a reconciliation. His letter of August, 1784, addressed the elder Franklin as "Dear and honoured father," and begged that they might "revive that affectionate intercourse and connexion which till the commencement of the late troubles had been the pride and happiness of my life."

Benjamin Franklin's reply stressed that "Indeed nothing has ever hurt me so much and affected me with such keen sensations, as to find myself deserted in my old age by my only son; and not only deserted, but to find him taking up arms against me, in a cause, wherein my good fame, fortune, and life were all at stake."

The two men met, briefly and awkwardly, several times in Paris. They talked stiffly but made little progress. Benjamin Franklin liked to stroll along the boulevards with his grandsons, but refused to be seen in public with William.

On January 1, 1788, Benjamin Franklin referred to the matter in a letter he wrote to the Rev. Dr. Byles of Boston. "My son is estranged from me by the part he took in the late war, and keeps aloof," he said. "The part he acted against me, which is of public notoriety, will account for my leaving him no more of an estate he endeavoured to deprive me of."

The estate to which Franklin referred was very large by today's standards. But at the death of the Sage of Philadelphia, his only son was left nothing but a barren tract of land in Nova Scotia plus "the books and papers in his possession." Embittered by his self-chosen exile, William Franklin died in England on November 17, 1813.

Though specialists in colonial history were aware of the bitter quarrel between father and son, the extent of Benjamin Franklin's emotional involvement was not discovered until recent times. In 1964 the Franklin Institute made public a long-lost will drawn up in 1757 when the Sage of Philadelphia was in New York waiting for passage to England. He prepared the document because of danger of attack at sea.

Income from Franklin's printing business, which yielded profits equivalent to more than $50,000 a year by modern standards, were in 1757 divided equally between Deborah Read, William Franklin, and Benjamin's daughter Sarah. But during the very period in which William was seeking reconciliation, his famous father drew up a new will leaving his son only a token inheritance.

General Jubal Early, Confederate States of America

While Jubal Early's Confederates Paused to Collect Ransom, Union Forces Strengthened the Defense of Washington

Carved out of semi-wilderness in order to become the site of a federal capital, the District of Columbia at first had a powerful geographical appeal. Even those delegates who wanted to establish the center of government in New York or Philadelphia conceded that the site favored by George Washington and destined to bear his name was about as close to the center of the new nation as one could hope it to be. Sixty years of westward expansion left the once-central capital dangling in the easternmost strip of the nation. Then secession drew east-west lines of such nature that Washington—dangerously close to Confederate soil—was too rich a prize for rebels to ignore.

Confederate General Jubal ("Jubilee") Early moved into the Shenandoah Valley in the spring of 1864 with the overt goal of stopping Union forces led by David F. Hunter. At Staunton, Virginia, men in blue who were commanded by Crook and Averell joined Hunter in order to form what seemed a nearly-invincible force of 18,000 seasoned men who sang of victory as they marched south.

Jubilee Early, with 30,000 men, moved out from Cold Harbor in time to be in position as Hunter's forces approached Lynchburg. Recognizing himself to be out-maneurvered and out-manned, the Union leader turned and retreated instead of making a full-scale attack. Later, Hunter lamely excused decisions that led to one of the most dramatic periods of the Civil War as having been occasioned by his lack of adequate ammunition.

He had enough firepower to pepper advancing Confederates and engage in frequent skirmishes. Still, Hunter led his men all the way through the long valley into the edge of West Virginia—with gray-clad troops close on his heels. The maneuver that Hunter described as "a strategic withdrawal" left Confederates clearly in command of the Shenandoah Valley—where any amateur could see that Washington was likely to become a target.

In spite of frantic telegrams from the capital, most troops racing to its defense were still days away. By Friday, July 8, only a motley group of raw short-term men under the command of General Lew Wallace stood between Early and the nerve center of the Union. On July 9th Early's men fought valiantly along the Monocacy River, thirty miles from Washington, but suffered 2000 casualties to 700 Confederate losses. The engagement ended not in a defeat, but in a rout.

According to contemporary accounts, "Terror gripped Washington City." Arms were issued to civilian employees of governmental agencies and rude fortifications were thrown up by untrained men. According to the *Independent Line,* "clerks of the Adjutant General's office were drilling in front of Lafayette Square, fully armed and equipped." Except for Major General Horatio Wright's VI Corps, there was no strong body of seasoned Union troops within the nation's capital.

Speculation—and rumor—abounded. Newspapers incorrectly estimated the strength of Early's forces at 45,000 veterans. Perhaps he would strike quickly in order to loot the federal treasury . . . or even to take Abraham Lincoln prisoner, and then withdraw. Or he might burn

Visiting McClellan's troops in Frederick, Md., Abraham Lincoln told cheering crowds that he hoped "Americans for a thousand generations will enjoy the blessings of a united nation."

and loot in the capital before pressing into southern Maryland to free 17,000 Confederates imprisoned at Point Lookout. Rumor, later verified, had it that through Horace Greeley, Lincoln had invited any citizen to step forward if he had a peace proposal whose only conditions would be restoration of the Union and abolition of slavery.

No one knows who spawned the idea that proved to keep rebel forces from penetrating Washington past the 7th Street line (well inside the District of Columbia). But someone—perhaps Early himself or one of his top aides—conceived the idea of "levying a contribution" instead of burning a captured Union city. Early's subordinate, John McCausland, demanded—and got—$20,000 on July 6 in return for sparing Hagerstown, Maryland, from the torch.

Defeat of Lew Wallace at the Monocacy River left a much finer plum in Confederate hands. Frederick, Maryland, with a population of about 8000, was a city by standards of the era. Many fine old buildings lined its streets; families who had gained their wealth from plantations and from commercial enterprises lived in mansions that helped to give Frederick its air of elegance.

Even though the federal dollar had shrunk in purchasing power to about thirty-nine cents, Confederates badly needed dollars for the purchase of war supplies in Europe. Jubilee Early demanded a "contribution" of $200,000 from citizens of Frederick. City fathers indicated eagerness to comply with his terms, but said they'd have to have time—at least twenty-four hours. Early pondered alternatives, decided to wait for the money instead of sacking the city, and duly collected the entire ransom.

While Early waited for his money, invalids and "hundred-day men" (drafted hurriedly for that period) were armed and organized. Federal troops began to reach the threatened city; some came up the Potomac by boat, others overland by forced march. Though many of them had never seen action, an estimated 20,000 soldiers in blue—greatly strengthened by being in a defensive rather than an offensive position—waited for Early and his men.

Confederates invaded the outer edges of Washington on July 11, but never made the major assault that was universally feared. The one-day delay brought about by the wait for Frederick's "contribution" was just enough to alter the balance of power. Confederates made a desultory attack upon Ft. Stevens while Lincoln was there to inspect the fortification. Oliver Wendell Holmes, Jr., twenty-three years old and unaware that he was destined to sit on the Supreme Court for nearly thirty years, shouted to the president: "Get down, you fool!"

That was as close as Jubilee Early came to getting his hands upon the President of the United States. Had he thrown his troops forward at full speed in the aftermath of crushing the forces of Lew Wallace, the history of the U.S. might have been different.

Maryland Senators Charles Mathias and J. Glenn Beall gave such weight to that crucial twenty-four-hour delay in Frederick that in 1970 they tried to get the federal government to reimburse the town that had saved Washington. At four percent interest, the original "contribution" of $200,000 would have swelled to about $6 million—a small price, they argued, for precious hours during which Union forces strengthened the defense of Washington.

Lawmakers from other regions opposed the restitution on the grounds that it would open a "Civil War pandora's box." Defeat of the bill for reimbursement of the city of Frederick relegated its all-important non-military action in the summer of 1864 to a lost page in American history.

The Atlanta Constitution *depicted President Hayes as an acrobat walking on the tips of bayonets*

Stolen Election Was Cinched Just Two Days Before Inauguration

A century ago, with inaugural ceremonies barely 48 hours away, Americans finally got the official word. After months of wrangling there was no longer any doubt that the popular-vote loser, Rutherford B. Hayes, would become 19th president.

Last-minute agreements by which the White House went to Hayes and the Republicans formalized the most flagrant theft of high office in our annals. Stolen electoral votes of Florida and South Carolina were decisive—and though they did get something, citizens of the southeast were big losers.

On November 8, 1876, headlines had proclaimed that the bitter contest was over. "TILDEN IS ELECTED," said the *New York Sun*. "COMPLETE DEMOCRATIC VICTORY," exulted the rival *Herald*. In Chicago the *Tribune* lamented: "TILDEN, TAMMANY AND THE SOLID SOUTH ARE TO RULE THE NATION."

With 4,300,590 votes against 4,036,298 for his opponent, Samuel J. Tilden had a clear mandate. But his solidly held 184 electoral votes fell just 1 short of the magic number needed for the presidency. Florida, Louisiana, South Carolina and Oregon still had not reported; electoral votes of only one of these would put Tilden at the nation's head. President U. S. Grant contemplated the dilemma and said that "Everything now depends upon a fair count" in states whose returns were late, and where challenges and counter-challenges were already surfacing.

A 4-month power struggle ensued. Before it ended it involved the sitting president, both houses of Congress, most members of the Supreme Court, scores of units of Federal troops, riots, and threats of renewed civil war. The backdrop against which the drama was played was the Civil War and subsequent "reconstruction" of the defeated South; federal troops were still stationed in South Carolina, Florida, and Louisiana.

Late on election night General Dan Sickles, who lost a leg at Gettysburg, was returning home from the theater. He stopped at Republican headquarters in New York City and found the place deserted because Tilden supporters were already celebrating victory. Republican National Chairman Zach Chandler had gone home, leaving word not to disturb him.

Supported by General Chester A. Arthur, Sickles drafted telegrams to Republican governors of 3 southern states—and sent them in Chandler's name. A few hours later Chandler was persuaded to follow with a message of hope for the party: "Hayes is elected if we have carried South Carolina, Florida, and Louisiana. Can you hold your state? Answer immediately." Before replies came Chandler began assembling delegations to go to these states with ample funds and code names under which to operate.

Since tallies would be challenged in each of the 3 vital southern states, President Grant entered the fray on November 10. He directed General William T. Sherman of "scorched earth" fame to use federal troops "to preserve peace and order during tabulation of votes."

South Carolina was already a battlefield. Governor Daniel H.

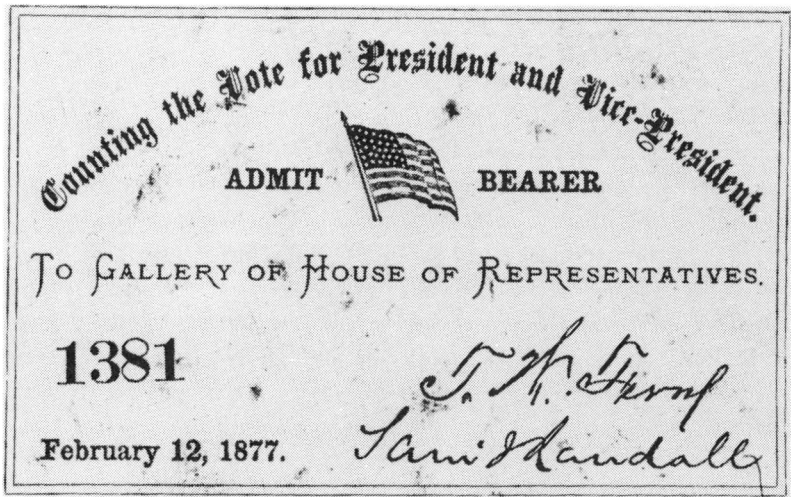

Admission ticket, gallery of the House of Representatives

Chamberlain, a carpetbagger who had come south to make his fortune, wanted more federal troops. Riots provided an excuse for using them. The worst of a series began in mid-September, spread over 5 counties and saw 10,000 armed men roaming the countryside. In July, 1875, South Carolina had been occupied by 10 companies of infantry and 2 batteries of artillery; the size of the federal contingent was tripled by election day, 1876.

After the vote both Chamberlain and his rival, Wade Hampton, claimed the State House. For a time South Carolina not only had 2 governors, but also 2 legislatures: one Republican, the other Democratic.

Florida saw less violence but at least as much manipulation of tallies as any other state. Manatee County went 10 to 1 for Tilden—and had its entire vote thrown out. Only 26 county returns went unchallenged. With 2 Republicans and 1 Democrat on the state canvassing board, Florida eventually gave Hayes the state by 45 votes (24,337 to 24,292).

Everywhere, there were rumors of resuming the Civil War. Federal troops were ordered to Washington from posts as distant as Leavenworth, Kansas. Units under Sherman's command were drilled daily in public streets. A heavily armed warship was anchored within sight of the Capitol. Some members of Congress strapped on side arms before going to sessions.

Committees named by the 2 houses of Congress to deal with electoral challenges were hopelessly deadlocked from the start. With both Republicans and Democrats fearful that Grant might remain in office past the expiration of his term unless a successor was inaugurated, a compromise—of sorts—was hammered out in January, 1877.

That compromise placed the fate of the White House in the hands of a special 15-member Electoral Commission having 5 members from the House, 5 from the Senate, and 5 from the Supreme Court. Democrats from the House were solidly behind Tilden; Republicans from the Senate were united in support of Hayes; 2 justices were Republicans, 2 were Democrats, and 1 was Independent.

Democrats depicted as threatening death to anyone voting for Hayes

David Davis of Illinois, the Independent on whom decisions of the commission were expected to hinge, was elected to the U. S. Senate by the Illinois Legislature on the very day that the Electoral Commission gained legal status. Since the high court had no other Independent, Davis' place was filled by Republican Joseph P. Bradley. As a result every vote taken by the Electoral Commission was 8 to 7 in favor of Hayes. Southerners used every possible delaying tactic and managed to prevent final action until Inauguration Day loomed at hand.

Southerners didn't abandon filibuster attempts until late February, after wide talk of a secret deal. Finally, on March 2 at 4:00 A.M. a joint session of Congress was informed that "Rutherford B. Hayes of Ohio, having received 185 electoral votes to Tilden's 184, is duly elected President of the United States for four years, commencing on the fourth day of March."

Southerners lost the White House. But because electoral votes of South Carolina and Florida had been yielded, federal troops were removed from the states so that the carpetbag era came to an end with the "Stolen Election."

William O. Stoddard's 1888 interpretation of "Vice-president Tyler Receiving the News of President Harrison's Death" —a widely circulated but highly improbable view
(wood engraving; Library of Congress)

In the Midst of Bitter Infighting among Whigs, Skinny John Tyler Literally Seized—and Kept—The White House

On September 17, 1787, thrity-nine delegates to the federal convention in Philadelphia approved and signed the United States Constitution. William Gladstone later called it "the most wonderful work ever struck off at a given time by the brain and purpose of man." But however able and dedicated the delegates were, many of them were bone-weary and eager to get a job done. Some later commentators upon their work have called it "a bundle of compromises and a mosaic of second choices."

If that verdict is too harsh, it is beyond dispute that framers of the Constitution failed in some instances to state their purposes—if, indeed, they had these purposes—in unequivocal language. So important was the office of president regarded that practically all of Article II was devoted to it. A single short paragraph dealt with the critical matter of a president's "death, resignation, or inability to discharge the powers and duties of the said office."

Should such a contingency arise—God forbid!—instructions for dealing with it were crammed into a single phrase: " . . . the same (power and duties of the said office) shall devolve on the vice-president."

In April, 1789, sixty-nine electors from ten states unanimously voted to place George Washington at the head of the new nation. Eight more presidents and fifty-two years later the unexpected happened; for the first time, a president died in office and it became immediately urgent to rally behind a successor.

John Tyler of Virginia occupied the place of vice-president largely because dominant men in the Whig party—and the rank and file of voters—regarded Tyler as harmless and the vice-presidency as an office with little honor and less power. Henry Clay and Daniel Webster were the two Whigs to watch. Both wanted and expected to win the presidency sooner or later; both had strong and vocal followings.

On inauguration day, 1841, Tyler took the oath of office first—in order to clear the decks for the really important ceremony, the inauguration of President Harrison. As soon as formalities were over and decency permitted, Tyler left the capital for his Williamsburg home: "very large and very airy and pleasant, fronting on a large lawn and surrounded by a most beautiful garden." Clearly he expected to spend most of the next four years in Williamsburg.

Just twenty days after he took office, Harrison suffered a severe attack of pneumonia. As his strength waned, it became apparent that he would die. No one thought it necessary to inform Tyler of the situation, however, Very early on the morning of April 5 he was awakened by loud banging on his front door. He went to the door in his nightshirt and admitted two couriers who informed him that President Harrison had died the day before. (The typically American legend that has the vice-president on his knees in the yard playing marbles with his son when he received the message, though widely circulated, is a folk myth without foundation.)

A terse written communication to Tyler from members of the cabinet addressed him, significantly, as "Mr. *Vice-President*." But one of the messengers was Daniel Webster's son Fletcher—who came in his capacity of chief clerk in the State Department. As clearly as anyone in the nation, Daniel Webster realized that his long-time rival, Henry Clay, now had an unmatched opportunity to move into the president's house for in the Whig convention of 1839, Clay had received 103 votes to Harrison's 94 on the first ballot. Webster had a strong following but had they been matched against one another then, Clay would have defeated the famous Massachusetts orator, hands down.

Precisely who chose Fletcher Webster to bear the news of Harrison's death to Tyler ambiguous records of the era do not say. But it was of crucial importance to Webster's ambitions that Tyler seize the presidency before Clay could lay claim to it. Hence it can hardly have been accidental or coincidental that Webster's son was sent to Williamsburg.

Within less than two hours after he got the news from Washington, Tyler was in the saddle for the first stage of his lightning-fast trip to the capital. Fletcher Webster and his companion as courier, a Mr. Beall who was on the payroll of the Senate, accompanied the vice-president. In Richmond, a special train was waiting. They reached Washington about 4 a.m. on April 6—and found the city buzzing with rumors and questions.

Tyler—who may have made up his mind independently or who may have been fed ideas and arguments by Fletcher Webster—acted promptly and decisively. At noon he went to the parlor of Brown's "Indian Queen" hotel and was sworn into the office of president by William Cranch, chief judge of the circuit court of the District of Columbia.

Whatever else may be concluded about the matter, this much is beyond dispute: no one had ever bothered seriously to try to determine whether death of a president in office should make the vice-president the chief executive, or merely an interim officer who would serve until a new president could be chosen. Language of the Constitution is ambiguous; "the same" may have meant to its framers the office of president, the duties of president—or both. Since the last surviving signer of the document had already died there was no one to question concerning the unwritten intent of its framers. With or without advice, Tyler had interpreted the document—and had acted in the light of his interpretation.

Henry Clay questioned the validity of Tyler's interpretation and was inclined to treat him as "acting president." In the House of Representatives, John McKeon of New York put in writing the question that was in every mind: "Is John Tyler entitled to the appellation 'President of the United States'?" Senator Allen of Ohio introduced a bill stipulating that in its communications with Tyler the lawmaking body should address him as "the Vice-president, on whom, by the death of the late President, the powers and duties of the office of President have devolved." Both legislative moves to depose Tyler failed, but many national leaders echoed the sentiments of ex-President John Quincy Adams who was insistent that "a strict construction (of the Constitution) would warrant more than a doubt whether the Vice-president has the right to occupy the President's house, or to claim his salary, without an Act of Congress."

Fifty-one-year-old Tyler, the youngest man who had so far assumed the office, made it clear that he had no intention to surrender it. "I am under providence made the instrument of a new test which is for the first time to be applied to our institutions," he wrote to Senator William C. Rives on April 9.

Vice-President Tyler's seizure of the nation's highest office, achieved with the encouragement and support of Daniel Webster, effectively settled the Constitutional question. In the light of the precedent he established, it became taken for granted that the vice president becomes chief executive when the highest office in the land is vacated by death or by resignation.

Presiding over the Supreme Court in a case that involved appointment of a justice of the peace, John Marshall made the Court the final interpreter of the U.S. Constitution

Awesome Power of the U.S. Supreme Court Was Largely Created by John Marshall in One Uncontested Ruling

Americans today take it for granted that the U.S. Supreme Court has absolute authority to decide what the Constitution means and what can or cannot be done as a result of that meaning. Founding fathers left no evidence whatever that they envisioned such a role for the judiciary body. It has come to be accepted because a single astute ruling by John Marshall, uncontested at the time, established the court he headed as interpreter of the Constitution.

Marshall's decision was a knock-out punch in a long and bitter political fight. From the perspective of nearly two centuries it is delightfully incongruous that the most important single ruling ever made by the Supreme Court was issued in the course of settling a dispute over the post of justice of the peace in the District of Columbia.

Defeat of John Adams and the Federalists in the election of 1800 added fuel to a fire already raging. Thomas Jefferson and the Democratic-Republicans would control the executive and legislative branches—but Adams had many weeks in which to strengthen already powerful Federalist forces within the judicial branch of the youthful nation.

Under Adams' prodding and coaxing, Congress provided for the appointment of sixteen new federal circuit judges—along with the necessary marshals and other officials. A separate statute empowered the president to name forty-two justices of the peace, who would be needed when the nation's capital moved from Philadelphia to the District of Columbia.

As yet the U.S. Supreme Court had little prestige. Justices were required to serve in federal circuit courts as well as the high court, to which only a trickle of cases went. Nothing in the Constitution prescribes the number of Supreme Court justices. Originally set at six by Congress, the number had been enlarged to seven in 1807. Fearing that the seat occupied by a justice about to retire would be filled by a Jeffersonian Republican, Adams persuaded Congress to sidestep that calamity by stipulating that when vacated the post would not be filled. As a final move aimed at political stalemate if not checkmate, when the Chief Justice offered his resignation because of "poor health" late in 1800 the president accepted it. Then he named his own Secretary of State—who had never held a judicial post—to the vacant seat. Instead of leaving the cabinet to assume the bench, John Marshall was for a short time both Secretary of State and Chief Justice.

March 3, 1801, was Adams' last day in the White House, He worked methodically until the very end, signing commissions. Most of them named Federalists to judicial posts ranging from federal circuits to J.P. courts in the District of Columbia. Signed commissions were sent to the State Department where Secretary of State John Marshall supervised the affixing of the great seal to each. All of the important ones were then delivered. But, somehow, Secretary of State Marshall failed to see that commissions reached newly-named justices of the peace.

A few hours later, Chief Justice John Marshall administered the oath of office to Jefferson. Within days the new president, already seething at the way in which Adams had packed the judiciary, learned that J.P. commissions signed by his predecessor had never been delivered. He therefore worked with his Attorney General, Levi Lincoln, to prepare a new and smaller list of appointees to capital posts. Instead of forty-two justices of the peace to function in the District of Columbia, Jefferson named thirty—half of whom were given authority in Alexandria County. Of the thirty he named, twenty-three came from the Adams list.

Most men nudged out of comfortable five-year posts because of Marshall's oversight and the coming of a new regime accepted their fate. Forty-one-year-old William Marbury did not. He enlisted three other "midnight judges," Messrs. Harper, Hooe, and Ramsay. With their backing, he filed suit aimed at requiring the new Secretary of State, James Madison, to deliver the commissions that had been signed by Adams late in his last night as president. The suit went to the Supreme Court, headed by John Marshall, under provisions of the Judiciary Act of 1789.

Jefferson and the Democratic-Republic Congress reacted to Adams' many judicial appointments swiftly and violently. The statute creating sixteen new federal circuits was repealed and appointees were left jobless. To prevent any abrupt action by the jurists whom Marshall headed, Congress abolished the last session of the Supreme Court scheduled to be held in Philadelphia and stipulated that the body would not again convene until February, 1801—in Washington.

Marbury vs. Madison, as the suit revolving about grievances of a would-be justice of the peace came to be called, seemed to offer two alternatives. The Supreme Court could bow to the power of the executive branch and declare the Jefferson commissions valid. Or the court could hold the Adams appointments to be binding—and watch, helpless to do anything, as Jefferson and his key men blithely ignored the ruling of the court.

Not yet seasoned in his judiciary role, John Marshall nevertheless groped for—and found—the Achilles' heel of his political rivals. Presiding over a Supreme Court made up only of himself, Justice Samuel Chase and Justice Bushrod Washington, Marshall personally hammered out a lengthy opinion that—on the surface—seemed to limit the authority of the judicial body.

William Marbury and his co-plaintiffs, said the decision, were as a matter of law entitled to their commissions. But the high court could do nothing on their behalf; the section of the Judiciary Act of 1789 under which they had brought action was unconstitutional. The case of *Marbury vs. Madison* was received by the Supreme Court on February 3; hearings concluded on February 14; Marshall handed down the verdict on February 24.

Nothing in the Constitution itself gave the Supreme Court authority to serve as the definitive interpreter. English common law, on which the whole edifice of American law was based, offered no precedent for Marshall's ruling. Yet it evoked no public outcry. Even Thomas Jefferson said nothing in public. Writing to Mrs. Adams many months later (in September, 1804) the chief executive did protest that "The opinion which gives to the judges the right to decide what laws are constitutional, and what not, . . . would make the judiciary a despotic branch."

Unchallenged and untested, the ruling stood. There would be no similar one for another fifty-four years. By then, time and precedent had done their work. Chief Justice Marshall, pondering issues in which Secretary of State Marshall had been deeply involved, had at one stroke effectively hamstrung both the legislative and the executive branches of the government in matters involving constitutionality.

Delivery of that stroke was made possible because otherwise-forgotten William Marbury refused to accept the verdict when informed that he would not receive his promised commission as justice of the peace.

Units of the 51st New York and 51st Pennsylvania made the first Union crossing of Antietam Bridge

A Soldier's Love for Tobacco Helped Union Forces Protect the U.S. Capital from Attack by Confederate Forces

By mid-September, 1862, most Americans knew that an all-important clash between Union and Confederate forces was in the making. His recent victory at Bull Run had convinced Robert E. Lee that this was the time to invade Maryland.

Several motives prompted such a military move. Maryland herself seemed to be swaying in the balance; she might throw her weight toward the Confederate side if captured. The state was rich in resources, and Lee's army was badly in need of provisions. Most important of all, Washington was within easy striking distance of strategic

KEY TO THE BATTLE OF ANTIETAM 39

Maryland sites. If the capital could be captured, Britain or France or both might enter the war on the Confederate side.

Lee's tired but confident columns moved into Maryland and occupied the town of Frederick without opposition. Cavalrymen under Wade Hampton were billeted in and about the community. Meanwhile, Lee dispatched a force of 25,000 men in gray to capture Harper's Ferry—vital to seizure of the Shenandoah Valley. Other large units of Confederate troops moved toward Hagerstown, Maryland.

Lee's opponent, McClellan, was notoriously slow and indecisive. It would not be too great a gamble, Lee reasoned, to disperse his troops in the best positions for offensive moves. An attack by slow-moving McClellan was practically unthinkable—totally out of character.

But a soldier's love for tobacco brought a sudden and dramatic change in the complex situation.

Men in blue moved into Frederick, Maryland, on September 12 only a few hours after Confederate forces evacuated the area. After breaking ranks and preparing to make camp in a field outside the town, men fighting to preserve the Union were permitted to fan out for a rest period. Two of them strolled along the edge of a field vacated a few hours earlier by their foes. As they walked, one spied what looked like a bundle of cigars.

Tobacco was already becoming scarce, so cigars would be a real prize. Seized and examined, the bundle was found to include "three good 'uns" that were wrapped in what appeared to be a letter. According to the wrapping paper, it had come from "Headquarters, Army of Northern Virginia" just three days earlier.

Tobacco-hungry soldiers temporarily lost interest in the weed. Scanning the document in which their cigars were wrapped they found it to be addressed to Major General D. H. Hill—and to be signed by Assistant Adjutant General R. H. Chilton. Hastily passed upward through the chain of command, the tobacco wrapper reached the tent of General George B. McClellan late in the afternoon. Aides familiar with Chilton's handwriting pronounced the document to be genuine—a copy of "Special Order #191" giving detailed instructions to Lee's scattered forces.

Few formal accounts of the Battle of Antietam give the tobacco wrapper more than passing attention. Brigadier General Willard Webb, for example, says only that "through fortuitous circumstances" McClellan learned where Lee's units were located and what they had been ordered to do.

Special Order #191, used by a tobacco-loving Confederate officer to protect three precious cigars and accidentally dropped where Union soldiers could find it, brought radical changes in McClellan. Contrary to what his own men as well as his opponents knew to be his pattern of action, he moved swiftly and decisively.

Attacking at several points simultaneously, the Union commander reached the main body of Lee's troops at a point where Antietam Creek flows through a ravine near the village of Sharpsburg. September 17, 1862, eventually entered history as "the bloodiest single day of the war." Neither force was able to give a precise account of losses, but by the most conservative estimates at least 25,000 men fell dead or wounded on that day.

Some units crossed the creek by means of an old stone bridge. Many more forded Antietam. Only the lucky few—such as men detailed to man observation towers some distance from the actual hand-to-hand fighting—spent the day without danger.

Military historians tend to label Antietam as "a drawn battle" or as "a defeat for both armies." But it was this battle that stopped Lee's move to encircle and capture Washington. Having repulsed the attempt at invasion, Union leaders could realistically claim a major victory. In the glow of that victory Abraham Lincoln issued the preliminary draft

Signal tower on Elk Mountain, overlooking Antietam Battlefield

Abraham Lincoln visited Antietam Battlefield in October, 1862

of the Emancipation Proclamation. Only a few weeks later he personally visited the battlefield where the surging lines of Confederates had been stopped.

Had tobacco-hungry men in blue not grabbed those three cigars, there would have been no Battle of Antietam. It was McClellan's use of the set of Confederate orders that brought forces into head-on conflict and elevation of Union morale because Lee had been stopped.

It took weeks for news of the standoff and of the resulting Emancipation Proclamation to reach Europe. Confederate leaders did not wait to receive dispatches couched in diplomatic language, but concluded that they must fight it out alone. For the night after paper used to wrap three precious cigars brought 110,000 men into hand-to-hand conflict, it was clear that there would be no Confederate triumph of such magnitude that foreign intervention would help to divide America into two separate nations.

Map was commissioned by England's famous Royal Society

Boundary Dispute Spawned North/South Dividing Line

After 12 days of impatient waiting, lookouts spotted sails of H.M.S. *Nanticoke*. Sure enough, her cargo included 20 carefully crafted slabs of oolitic limestone. Quarried and cut in Portland, England, each marker bore a carved *P* on one side and a carved *M* on the opposite face. A few days later, in mid-December, 1765, H.M.S. *Choptank* docked with another 30 slabs. This time, nearly half bore the coat of arms of the Penns on one side, and that of the Baltimores on the other.

Too bad. With winter at hand the stones could not be used. There was nothing to do but wait. March 15, 1766, brought a break in the weather. Charles Mason and Jeremiah Dixon superintended the loading of their precious telescope and surveyor's instruments on a 1-horse

THE MASON-DIXON LINE

chair with springs—and as an extra precaution padded the bed of the vehicle with a feather bed. With their precious 12"-square limestone markers in hand they were ready to establish a permanent line.

Astronomer Charles Mason and mathematician-surveyor Jeremiah Dixon hadn't sought the job. Charles Bradley, Britain's Astronomer Royal, had specifically recommended them. He did so at the urgent request of Lord Baltimore plus Richard and William Penn. Heirs of the founders of Maryland and of Pennsylvania had been at odds for 82 years because chaotic colonial charters were incredibly inexact. Maryland's land claims included the city of Philadelphia, while Baltimore lay within the tract claimed by Pennsylvania.

Three times adjudicated by British courts, legal settlements had not been accepted by disputing parties. Attempts to get an exact survey of the disputed territory had been futile. America had plenty of surveyors—including young Lt. Colonel George Washington and attorney Thomas Jefferson. But only Englishmen, agreed the absentee landlords, had the skill to run a true line through the wilderness. That's why they requested and got recommendations from the Astronomer Royal.

Already, the impatient heirs to land that only one of the 3 had ever seen had agreed upon terms of settlement—contingent upon an accurate survey. Their Indenture of Agreement, signed on July 4, 1760, omitted no detail; as printed in the *Pennsylvania Archives* it runs to 36 pages of fine type. Three years later, on July 20, 1763, they accepted as the Pennsylvania-Maryland boundary whatever line Messrs. Mason and Dixon might establish.

Mason had won his reputation as an astronomer; as chief of the surveying party he kept a daily log. Lost for decades, it was found at Halifax, Nova Scotia, in 1860. Bought for the U. S. Department of State for $500 in gold, it now rests in our National Archives in Washington. From this bulky record, alone, practically the full story of the 18th-century survey can be reconstructed.

Axmen felled trees and heavy bushes to clear a path 10' to 12' wide. Using astronomical observations to establish a starting point, the expedition headed by Mason and Dixon moved ever-so-slowly westward. A limestone post was set up at each 1-mile interval; every 5th post bore the arms of the litigants. Four years and 233 weary miles from their starting point the surveyors faced so many hostile Indians that they called quits.

Much to their gratification, both Lord Baltimore and the grandsons of William Penn accepted the results of the survey and petitioned the King in Council to ratify their pact. By it the Pennsylvania-Maryland boundary dispute was finally settled; Maryland lost about 4,300 square miles as a result. Mason and Dixon submitted their final bill, in amount £3,512/9s. Simultaneously they collected from England's Royal Society £200 for moonlighting as astronomers while making their survey.

Since all parties to the transaction, including the Royal Society, expressed their complete satisfaction, the whole business should have ended then and there. That it did not is due chiefly to the fact that the dividing line between colonies established by Mason and Dixon constituted North America's first truly accurate long-distance survey. Running a few seconds past 39° 43' north latitude, it was accepted as a bench mark from which to measure distances both north and south. Extended many miles to the west in 1784, it was found "without important error" in re-surveys of 1849 and 1900.

Because the Pennsylvania-Maryland boundary was known to be precise, in everyday life the line moved forward across the U. S. map as the frontier pushed westward. That's how it came to be mentioned with increasing frequency as debates over the boundary between free and slave territory opened up. Though the extended Mason-Dixon Line of 1784 stopped at Pennsylvania's southwestern corner, it was natural to treat the Ohio River as a continuation of it.

Everything below this now-meandering Mason-Dixon Line became "the south"; every point above it was regarded as "the north." With two distinctly different legal and social entities having been created, it was perhaps inevitable that north and south should eventually go to war.

That pair of experts from overseas who worked during the 1760's would have turned over in their graves had they been capable of hearing guns that fired upon Ft. Sumter. For the line that was created by Mason and Dixon is British — not American — from stem to stern. British patricians quarreled over a boundary line. A British scientist recommended two British experts to survey that line. In their work the surveyors used British instruments and set up mileposts cut from British stone. Results of their work were made formal by a decree from a British monarch.

Steamer LEXINGTON as depicted in "The Extra Sun," lithograph by Currier

A Forgotten Disaster Was the Springboard that Enabled Currier & Ives to Leap into the Place of "Printmakers to the American People"

Except to serious collectors of prints the name "Currier & Ives" is likely to suggest gentle pastoral scenes, celebrities of a bygone era, fine horses and elegant clipper ships. The firm's own "Catalogue of Popular Cheap Prints containing nearly Eleven hundred subjects" listed additional categories: "Juvenile, Domestic, Love Scenes, Kittens and Puppies, Ladies Heads, Catholic Religious, Patriotic, Landscapes, Vessels, Comic, School Rewards and Drawing Studies, Flowers and Fruits, Motto Cards, Horses, Family Registers, Memory Pieces and Miscellaneous in great variety."

45

That bland list gives no hint that Nathaniel Currier began depicting disasters very early or that he was propelled into the national limelight through skillful—and astute—exploitation of the 1840 loss of the steamer *Lexington* in Long Island Sound.

Regarded as a marvel of the shipbuilding art when she was launched in 1835, the *Lexington*—all 205 feet of her—came into existence through the bustling genius of Cornelius Vanderbilt. Because he operated a fleet of passenger ships Vanderbilt was dubbed "Commodore" in 1837 by the *Journal of Commerce*—a title that stuck to him when he turned from water to the rails.

The *Lexington* involved a major gamble for the boat owner who was eager to become a business tycoon. Passenger business between New York and Providence, Rhode Island, was a virtual monopoly of the wealthy and powerful Boston and New York Transportation Co. To challenge it, Vanderbilt went in hock for all he had, built the 488-ton *Lexington*, and advertised her as "the fastest boat in the world." She did make sixteen miles an hour under good weather conditions, and gave established lines real trouble. To stifle competition from a third line, the Atlantic Steamboat Co., the Boston-based firm offered to give Vanderbilt a profit of nearly $20,000 if he would sell his fine, fast vessel. Had Vanderbilt not taken that 1839 offer, he might have died unknown. For direct losses plus lawsuits resulting from the *Lexington* tragedy amounted to more than $2,000,000—many times Vanderbilt's assets in 1840.

Bound for Stonington, Connecticut, with a crew of forty and about one hundred passengers, the *Lexington* left New York on the evening of January 13, 1840. Fire broke out as the vessel nosed through Long Island Sound. Crewmen turned back toward the pier, but the fire was raging out of control while the *Lexington* was still two miles from land. A few persons managed to stay afloat on bales of cotton that had constituted the cargo. But an estimated 136 burned to death or perished in the icy water.

Just three days after the tragedy New Yorkers were offered a chance to buy a lithograph print of the burning ship accompanied by seven columns of description in fine print. Termed "The Extra Sun" and issued under auspices of The New York *Sun* it is widely regarded as the first illustrated extra in history. Buyers who were impressed by the vivid illustration that headed the page could look beneath it and discover that it was drawn by W. K. Hewitt and produced by "N. Currier, Lith. & Pub. 2 Spruce St. N.Y."

Colored litho prints of the burning of New York's famous Crystal Palace on October 5, 1858, were just 6¢ per copy, wholesale, from the firm that started a national sales program with a disaster and depicted a great many notable ones

"The Extra Sun" was first a local and then a national triumph. Profits from it gave Currier the opportunity he had been seeking to distribute his prints on a more than local basis. Publicity about it assured him of a market for whatever he could produce.

Currier's move to capitalize on the disaster did not occur in a vacuum. Already the Massachusetts native who had learned the trade as an apprentice in Boston had discovered that there is money in violent death. Two of his earliest surviving prints, both uncolored, had enjoyed local success. One of them shows "Ruins of the Planters Hotel, New-Orleans, Which fell at two O'clock, on the Morning of the 15th of May 1835, burying 50 persons, 40 of which escaped with their Lives." Another depicts "Ruins of the Merchant's Exchange, N.Y., after the Destructive Conflagration of Decbr. 16 & 17, 1835."

Compared with "The Extra Sun" these and all earlier Currier prints were small-time stuff. A biographer of the printer may have been overenthusiastic in declaring that "overnight N. Currier became a national institution," but there's no doubt that his illustrated account of the burning of the *Lexington* put him head and shoulders above all competitors who operated on a local basis.

Nathaniel's brother Charles worked with him for a period. Then Charles' brother-in-law, native New Yorker James M. Ives, entered the business a decade after publication of "The Extra Sun." Ives soon became a full partner and the firm name was changed to the universally familiar "Currier & Ives."

Black-and-white prints produced by means of a special kind of soft and very porous stone imported from Bavaria were hand-tinted by crews of women who worked on long waist-high tables. Production costs were kept so low that except for special editions and large folio prints the typical product that bore the "Currier & Ives" imprint was sold at about 6¢, in quantity.

For more than half a century, Currier & Ives prints depicted every aspect of life in America. Though not given a separate section in the publishers' catalog, many best-sellers capitalized on the news value of shipwrecks, fires, train wrecks, and other disasters.

Development of photography and photoengraving gave Currier & Ives little trouble at first. But as the arts progressed and illustrated weeklies began to be widely distributed, hand-tinted lithographed prints became harder and harder to sell. Hundreds of thousands of them were discarded as trash before they began to be collectors' items early in this century. By 1928 one rare print depicting "The Life of a Hunter—A Tight Fix" was worth $3,000.

Widely known as "Printmakers to the American Nation," Currier & Ives didn't keep precise records. No one knows how many separate prints they issued, but the number is believed to range above or below 4000. Only harum-scarum Charles, Nathaniel's brother and part-time business colleague bothered to keep specimens of a majority of the later prints. He did it because he had convenient storage space for proofs.

In a unique sense, Currier & Ives prints *are* 19th-century America. Proud owners of prints that show trotting horses, Biblical scenes, and the American countryside might never have had an opportunity to acquire them had not the *Lexington* gone down in flames.

President Grover Cleveland—who won the White House in spite of scandals greater than those that have defeated other aspirants

Three Separate Stains on His Record, Each Enough to Keep a Man Out of the White House, Failed to Stop Grover Cleveland

Stephen Grover Cleveland was practically unknown nationally when Democrats nominated him for president in July, 1884. Meeting at Exposition Hall in Chicago, jubilant delegates dubbed the man they chose on the second ballot as "Grover the Good."

But because they had made only the most perfunctory inquiry into his background, elation of Democratic leaders was short-lived. In quick succession the man who had stepped into the limelight was confronted by three separate stains on his record.

Son of a Presbyterian minister, Cleveland was born on March 18,

1837, in Caldwell, New Jersey, as the fifth of nine children. His father got the job of district secretary for the American Home Missionary Society, which required the family to move to the village of Holland Patent in central New York. At sixteen Grover, who had already stopped using his first name, was thrown on his own by the death of his father.

He went to New York City job hunting, and for a time worked at a school for the blind. Then he got a post as clerk in a Buffalo law firm. He studied at night, sometimes without sleeping at all, and learned enough law to win admission to the bar in 1859.

He was moderately successful as an attorney, but when the post of sheriff of Erie County became vacant in 1870 he ran for the job. "No other lawyer would have considered the post suitably dignified for his talents," a local newspaper editorial commented in reporting that the attorney had won by 303 votes.

After three years as sheriff Cleveland joined the firm of Bass and Bissell and again became a full-time lawyer. He nearly doubled his weight from beer and sausages at Schenkelberger's Restaurant. Civic corruption encouraged him to run for mayor in 1881. He won, and established a local reputation as a reformer. This gave him a base from which to win the governorship of New York in 1882.

Two years later Republicans chose as their national standard-bearer James G. Blaine of Maine. He would be difficult if not impossible to beat. Democrats, who decided that their best hope lay in "a new face," rallied to the support of Cleveland as "a man who has never even set foot in Washington."

Within ten days after being nominated, Cleveland moved from obscurity into national notoriety.

Republicans had no difficulty digging out his record as sheriff of Erie County—and learning that he had presided over the executions of condemned killers Patrick Morrissey and Jack Gaffney. Regardless of offenses committed by the executed men, two hangings were enough to serve as a hook on which to display the emotion-charged label: "The Hangman."

While broadsides about "The Hangman" were still being printed and distributed a second scandal broke over the head of the man who hadn't really sought the nomination. In its issue of July 21, 1884, the Buffalo, New York *Evening Telegram* gave front-page space to "A Terrible Tale."

According to that tale, the candidate for the presidency had long been involved with Maria Halpin. "A child was born out of holy wedlock," readers were informed. "Now ten years of age, this sturdy lad is named Oscar Folsom Cleveland. He and his mother have been supported in part by our ex-mayor who now aspires to the White House. Astute readers may put the facts together and draw their own conclusions."

When the story broke, frantic Democratic leaders wired Cleveland for instructions. His telegram became a classic document in American politics. "Tell the truth!" Cleveland said.

The truth, it developed, was that Cleveland and other men had visited Maria Halpin regularly. As the only bachelor in the group Cleveland took financial responsibility for the child. "The boy could be mine," he confessed, "I do not know." National Music Co. of Chicago promptly published and Republican money subsidized mass distribution of a song unique in the annals of American politics. "Ma! Ma! Where's My Pa?" made it impossible for any informed voter to be unaware of scandal in Cleveland's past.

Just to make sure that the big man was properly polished off, opponents dragged a third skeleton out of his closet. Called to the colors to help save the Union, Cleveland had resorted to provisions of the Conscription Act of 1863. Under its terms he had paid $150 for a substitute who would wear Union blue—while he remained in his handsome residence and office building.

Cleveland made no serious national effort to inform voters that at the time he bought his way out of the army he already had two brothers in uniform—plus a mother and two sisters at home to support. His indifference to the charge was characteristic. Unlike modern candidates, he never mounted a serious campaign. He made few public appearances and fewer speeches. While charges echoed and re-echoed, he stayed at his desk in Albany and looked after his work as governor.

Experts on both sides conceded that New York was the pivotal state—and scandals were expected to beat him there. That might have been the case had not political foes made one last effort to milk the paternity issue for all it was worth. Just a week before the election Blaine himself went to New York City and met with clergymen who were already indignant that a man so stained as Cleveland might become president.

Buffalo, New York, residence and law office of Grover Cleveland, Esq.

The Rev. S. D. Burchard, pastor of Murray Hill Presbyterian church, was spokesman for the clergy. While reporters jotted down notes he talked earnestly with Blaine. In the midst of the conversation he referred to the Democratic Party as "the party of Rum, Romanism, and Rebellion." Blaine made no objection to the allusion.

"Rum, Romanism, and Rebellion" made headlines in most New York papers on October 29 and 30, however. Angry Irish Catholics turned out in record numbers to repudiate the man who had permitted a slur at their faith. Ten days after the election Republican leaders conceded defeat; Cleveland had carried New York State (and hence the nation) by 1149 popular votes. Nationally he had less than fifty percent of the votes in the four-way race, but in the electoral college he took 219 votes to Blaine's 182.

Outcome of the hotly-contested election was apparent on the day Blaine's forces conceded that the "Rum, Romanism, and Rebellion" reference had brought out enough angry Catholics to swing the national contest. On learning that his opponents had finally conceded, the candidate plagued by scandal admitted reporters to his Albany office. "I am glad they have conceded," the big man said. "Very glad. There will be no trouble. If they had not conceded, I should have felt it my duty to take my seat anyhow."

The Selden Motorcar—built as a model early in this century and later given a backdated painted label—had a 2-cylinder, 4-cycle motor

George B. Selden: The Lawyer Who Patented the Automobile

New York attorney George Baldwin Selden (1846-1922) never actually invented anything. But he had a keen imagination and was a good authority on patent law. As a result he managed to gain a legal monopoly on the manufacture of automobiles in the U.S. It held up long enough for him to collect at least $1,500,000 in royalties. Then it was challenged by hard-headed young Henry Ford of Detroit, who broke the monopoly during the years he was surging to first place among automakers.

Discharged from the Union Army in 1865, 19-year-old Selden had

53

entered Yale Sheffield Scientific School, but during his second year his father's illness forced him to drop out of school. Reluctantly he decided to follow in his father's footsteps and hang out his shingle as a lawyer.

Admitted to the bar in 1871, young Selden continued to tinker with mechanical contrivances such as those he had studied in engineering school. Beginning in 1875, he designed several types of engines; none worked.

Petroleum technicians were just beginning to achieve success in separating the liquid into specific fractions. Selden decided that one of the fractions was the fuel of the future—and that he must have a monopoly on "gasoline road locomotives." His decision was triggered by a visit to the Philadelphia Centennial Exposition of 1876. There he saw a two-cycle gasoline motor, designed and patented by George B. Brayton.

Selden knew enough law—and engineering—to believe that a three-cycle motor would get around the Brayton patent. So he returned to Rochester and had a 600-pound engine built. To save time and money, only one of the three cylinders was bored and fitted with a piston. Theoretically, though, the "Selden engine" ought to operate at 500 rpm as opposed to 25 rpm for the Brayton engine.

By 1877, Selden was ready to make his first legal move. He drew a sketch of a gasoline-powered vehicle with a crude friction clutch and a system for changing gears.

U.S. law of the era provided that the holder of a patent was entitled to a monopoly during a period of seventeen years. There was no provision for renewal. Since no one was actually building and selling automobiles based on the Selden concept, it would have been a mistake to take out a patent too early. George Selden waited almost two years before he even applied for a patent. Once the application was on file, he began adding new claims. When patent examiners disallowed a particular claim, he was given two years to alter his application—and add more claims. Until a patent was actually granted, only the applicant and the U.S. Patent Office knew anything about it. But date of the first application was used in establishing priority. George Brayton, inventor of the engine that Selden modified slightly, later said of his competitor: "He was a punk engineer—but a damned smart patent lawyer! He knew exactly what to do and, when."

1894 was a break-through year. The world's first automobile race was run from Paris to Rouen. Publicity about it helped to convince many members of the public that the horseless carriage, which had run eighty miles at ten miles per hour, might really make a go of it.

It was time to quit stalling, Selden decided. He abandoned legal maneuvers and asked the U.S. Patent Office to give him a seventeen-year monopoly on the manufacture and sale of gasoline-powered vehicles. Patent #549,160 was issued on November 5, 1895. A few months later Charles and Frank Duryea claimed the first U.S. commercial sale of a horseless carriage powered by gasoline.

During this era the world's largest maker of bicycles was the Pope Manufacturing Co. of Hartford, Connecticut. Col. Albert A. Pope, self-made millionaire who owned the company and the trademark "Columbia," calculated that in time the horseless carriage might cut into the bicycle market. So he decided to build and market a car that he would call "Columbia."

Pope hired a bright young engineer named Hiram Percy Maxim (1869-1936) and told him to put crews to work in order to get gasoline-powered vehicles into production. By 1897, ten Columbias were in various stages of completion.

It was then that a member of Colonel Pope's legal department discovered that they were too late. "A man named Selden has already won a patent," he told his employer. "I have checked the records carefully. He has an airtight case. We could fight, but we couldn't win."

Pope had made his millions by shrewd moves that included the principle, "If you can't lick your foes, then join them." He sent for Selden, worked out an agreement by which the all-inclusive patent would be assigned to a holding company in return for a percentage of all royalties collected.

Pope had the right connections to make a go of the Electric Vehicle Company. Stockholders who bought into it included some of America's top financiers. William C. Whitney, former Secretary of the Navy and a noted capitalist, was among the first to enter the company. He was joined by Thomas F. Ryan of New York and P. A. B. Widener of Philadelphia. Both men were already prominent as electric traction magnates. New York banker Anthony M. Brady provided more capital.

Once the Electric Vehicle Company gained rights to the Selden patent, officials announced that all gasoline-powered cars made in the U.S. would have to be built by license—accompanied by royalties of

5% of retail price. Suits against the Buffalo Gasoline Motor Company and the Automobile Fore-carriage Co. were won easily. Sued for infringement of the Selden patent, the big and growing Winton Motor Carriage Co. capitulated and took a consent decree.

Repeatedly sustained in courts, the Selden interests clearly had the U.S. auto industry by the tail. Firms licensed to operate under the Selden patent formed the Association of Automobile Makers. Every car produced carried a plate acknowledging that it was made by license.

Practically all manufacturers joined the Association—but one stubbornly refused to do so. Henry Ford, head of the hold-out organization, was just sixteen at the time attorney George Selden filed his preliminary application for a patent in 1879. Suit was filed against Ford's company on October 22, 1903, in the Southern District of New York.

It looked like an open-and-shut case. Members of the Association of Automobile Makers represented more than $70,000,000 in capital assets. During 1903, Ford's working capital was just under $30,000.

Both parties to the suit began taking out newspaper and magazine advertisements while the case was being fought. A full-page ad in *The*

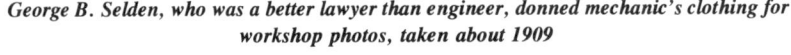

George B. Selden, who was a better lawyer than engineer, donned mechanic's clothing for workshop photos, taken about 1909

Automobile warned that "the basic Selden patent will be enforced against all infringers." Meanwhile, The Ford Motor Co. bought space to tell prospective dealers, users, and exporters: "We will protect you against all prosecution from alleged infringements. No court in the U.S. has ever decided in favor of the patent; all that has been done is to record a prior agreement between parties."

Litigation dragged out for a period of six years. Testimony in the case filled thirty-six volumes. In September, 1909, the court of New York's Southern District upheld the Selden patent. This verdict was based, in part, upon physical examination of a car hastily manufactured by engineer Henry Cave—who worked from Selden's initial drawings. The gasoline vehicle he made never ran more than fourteen hundred feet. Boldly labelled "1877" in spite of having been put together more than thirty years after that date, it helped to sway judicial opinion.

Federal Judge Charles M. Hough, who handed down the ruling supporting the claims of Selden, said that "this American patent represents a great idea shaped in 1879, which lay fallow in a Patent Office file wrapper until 1895."

Henry Ford promptly appealed the decision. During the two years in which arguments were being heard, the Detroit manufacturer's arguments with Selden interests were repeatedly aired in the press. In all history, no patent fight has been given so much free coverage.

January, 1911, brought the case to a close. Selden's patents were still valid, the courts declared. But his combination of engine, running gear, clutch, and other components did not cover the "modern" automobile. That meant that the Model T did not represent an infringement upon the patent covering a car never manufactured.

Attorney Selden was not greatly disturbed. His monopoly had just one more year to run. Royalties from a paper invention had made him comfortable for life. Consequently the attorney rejected suggestions that the case be taken to the Supreme Court. Until the end of his life, in 1922, his investments returned more than adequate income for his needs. He died insisting that though he never actually built an automobile, he was the inventor of "the idea of the gasoline-propelled vehicle."

The ghost of Charles I, as depicted in a 1659 pamphlet, may have tormented the "regicides" who escaped to the New World—but if so, they failed to show remorse

For 20 Years, Pious New England Puritans Sheltered Fugitives in an International Manhunt

During 17th-century civil wars in England, the victory of Oliver Cromwell made King Charles I a political prisoner. Recaptured after an escape that may have been engineered by Cromwell himself, the king was brought before a High Court of Justice whose members were so biased that they constituted a rigged jury. Some balked at putting their ex-king to death, but fifty-nine followers of Cromwell put their names to the death warrant.

Failure of Cromwell's Commonwealth and restoration of the monarchy brought inevitable retaliation against the regicides—whom the new Parliament branded as "unpardonable." Each man held responsible for the death of Charles was subject to being hanged, or drawn and quartered while still alive. With a price upon his head, every fugitive was a prototype of the 20th-century war criminal—safe nowhere, and doomed to live in hiding for the remainder of his days.

Three of these wanted men fled to New England and found sanctuary among pious Puritans. Throughout the region there was an unwritten conspiracy to shelter the regicides—in the name of God and at the risk of being seized and condemned as a traitor to the crown. At least one colonial governor was a party to the plot. The Rev. Increase Mather of Boston's North Church plunged into it with such holy zeal that he served as intermediary through whom code letters were exchanged between fugitives and their loved ones in England. Spurning the bounty offered by agents of King Charles II and risking their own lives by harboring fugitives, Puritans stuck together so closely that all three regicides who fled to the colonies died of natural causes.

Years earlier, in England, only a handful of persons were really eager to see Charles' head roll. Many who helped to unseat him from the throne would have been satisfied to see him banished to a land where he could do no harm, or at most confined in a comfortable prison for life. Oliver Cromwell wrestled with the issue and concluded that in order to make the world safe for the "Saints" of whom he was chief, the ex-monarch must die. Publicly, he asked his followers to wait patiently for a sign from God.

Ten days after Cromwell included such a plea in his speech to the Army Council on November 1, 1647, Charles escaped from Hampton Court where he had been under detention. Edward Whalley, commander of a regiment of horse and first cousin to Cromwell, was responsible for guarding the king. Much evidence, including a letter from Cromwell to Whalley, suggests that his captors deliberately permitted the monarch to escape in order to find a temporary haven on the Isle of Wight.

Now Cromwell had his sign from heaven! Now he had an issue on which to base his demand that Charles be tried for his life. Writing to Lord Wharton on January 1, 1651, Cromwell urged: "Be not offended at the manner of God's working; perhaps no other way was left." That constituted a theological argument after-the-fact; Charles had been dead for nearly two years.

Though the special High Court of Justice that heard the case against the king included 135 men, only 59 of them signed the death warrant. Cromwell's cousin was the fourth man to sign. William Goffe, son-in-law of Whalley and like him a major general who commanded a district of the Commonwealth, was fourteenth to sign. Two-thirds of the way down the list appeared the signature of John Dixwell.

Almost as soon as Charles was dead, the rank and file of Englishmen began to realize that with Cromwell at the head of the nation they had merely exchanged one harsh master for another. An informal program of beatification began, with the result that before he had been in his grave a decade the once-hated Charles I was revered as a sainted martyr.

This reversal of public opinion strengthened the hand of those who itched to topple Cromwell from power and of those who yearned for the good old days of monarchy. From his self-imposed exile Charles II crystallized national opion by declaring for a free Parliament and issuing a proclamation of General Amnesty. Under its terms, if made king he would punish no one except persons specified by Parliament.

When in 1660 it became clear that the monarchy would be restored, one-time major generals Edward Whalley and William Goffe managed to gain passage on the *Prudent Mary*—whose destination was the colonies. John Dixwell fled to the continent, remained in hiding there for a time, and then joined his comrades who were comfortably established in New England.

Over and over, officers of the crown sent their men on forced marches when they got wind of the whereabouts of one or more of the fugitives. Over and over, God-fearing and law-abiding Puritans hid the regicides, fed and clothed them, and helped them to find new havens. Though broadsides and proclamations repeatedly emphasized that there was a reward of £100 per man offered for the regicides, no colonist seems ever to have attempted to turn bounty hunter.

All three men used false names at times, but identities of all three were known to prominent men in Massachusetts and in Connecticut. Their New World hosts gave aid and comfort to the wanted men "for conscience' sake." They did it with such zealous effectiveness that John Dixwell, youngest of the fugitives and last to die, married twice and sired at least three children before his death at age eighty-one.

Dixwell was buried in New Haven close to the spot where Yale was later founded; his grave was marked with a stone that bore his initials. Goffe vanished for good during a 1679 manhunt; his father-in-

As he went to his execution on January 30, 1649, pious captors of Charles I informed him that "God did not wish him to escape"

law had already died of natural causes and had been buried in an unmarked grave.

Not even the long arm of the English king and the awesome power of his redcoats and colonial officers could shake the solidarity of Puritan New England. A twenty-year international manhunt for men condemned as murderers of Charles I failed to flush even one of the three into the hands of the law.

The 21-Year-Old Who Discovered a Continent

In November, 1820, the captain of a U.S. sealing ship discovered the Continent of Antarctica. It had been hunted for 200 years by veteran explorers—but at the time he made the find, Nathaniel Brown Palmer was just twenty-one years old.

Born in Stonington, Connecticut, on August 8, 1799, young Palmer practically grew up in his father's shipyard. At age fourteen Nat went to sea—as a blockade runner in the War of 1812. Three years later the boy whose acquaintances said "he had salt water in his veins" had become second mate of a deep-sea vessel. A year later, at age eighteen, Palmer got his own command—the schooner *Galena*.

Stonington was then the world center of the seal trade. At first casually and experimentally, New England whalers had begun to kill and skin a few of the animals. Pelts brought about $2 each. Even a small vessel could bring back 8,000 to 10,000 pelts, though. So sealing surged to prominence. Persons who invested in a successful voyage could expect profits ranging as high as 800 percent.

Fast growth in sealing, which involved Britain and Russia as well as the U.S., led to a rapid decline in the number of seals that lived in the old, established rookeries. This factor spurred an intensive search for a new source of seals.

For more than 200 years seamen had talked vaguely of a "Lost Aurora" believed to lie somewhere south of Cape Horn. Captain James

Cook and other noted explorers had spent months hunting for the semilegendary land, but none had succeeded in setting foot upon it.

Shrewd Yankee investors of Stonington reasoned that many seals must breed in regions south of islands that appeared on conventional navigational charts. In order to search for such islands, Connecticut businessmen outfitted their first voyage to search for Lost Aurora in 1817.

One of the men who made that voyage—which proved fruitless in terms of major discoveries—was Nathaniel Palmer. He went as second mate of the brig *Hersilia*. The post, which involved a demotion in rank, was taken because good prospects of a huge seal kill, with bounty to match, offered bigger reward than conventional captain's pay.

The *Hersilia* found no new land—but brought back to Stonington more than 10,000 prime pelts. Merchants and seamen of the city decided to send a much larger expedition into the general vicinity of the South Shetland Islands. By standards of the era, the expedition that left Stonington on July 31, 1820, was a huge convoy. Five brigs were included, along with three schooners.

As an extra precaution investors had commissioned the building of a special shallow-draft sloop. This forty-five ton vessel, about forty-seven feet long, had a draft of just six feet. She stood so low in the water that her decks were washed by waves more than eighteen inches high. Dubbed *Hero*, this sloop was something of an experiment in both shipbuilding and in sealing. Designed to serve as scout for the entire flotilla, the vessel could safely explore coastal regions in which ships of conventional build were likely to founder or to become stuck.

Nat Palmer, commander of the *Hero*, had just six men in his crew, but was assured of a captain's share of prize money from the sealing expedition. Along with other vessels of the Yankee flotilla, the *Hero* reached the South Shetland Islands in early November, but found no seals. Logs of the Stonington ships, carefully perused decades later, indicated that skippers believed sealers of other nations beat them to the region and had taken pups as well as adult seals.

There were two choices: go home empty, or look elsewhere. Captains held a council of war and decided that the big ships would wait while the *Hero* explored uncharted waters farther south.

November 16 saw the tiny sloop reach Deception Island—known by name to some navigators, but shunned because heavy fog made the waters dangerous. Palmer's shallow-draft vessel entered a previously unknown "spacious harbor with very deep water" that is now known to be the crater of an extinct volcano. Probably from the top of the mast of the tiny *Hero*, on a day "surprisingly clear," twenty-one-year-old Nathaniel Palmer was "thrown into great excitement upon seeing to the south a vast extent of land."

By late evening on the following day, November 17, the little sloop from Connecticut was close to what is now known as Trinity Island. The water, "filled with immense Ice Bergs," was extremely dangerous. Early next morning the youthful skipper guided his craft ten miles into a strait "tending SSW and NNE and Literally filled with Ice and the shore inaccessible."

Palmer, whose notes in the log are unusually terse, commented only that "We thought it not Prudent to venture farther . . . for everywhere, the shore was Perpendicular." The Stonington youth had no idea that he had discovered the last of the world's continents, or that its 5,000,000 square miles harbored penguins and other strange creatures—with ice perhaps covering vast treasures in oil and minerals.

Palmer went back to the sealing squadron and soon afterward led other ships into a bay in the Greenwich Islands, where seals were found in abundance. Again out scouting a few weeks later, on February 5, 1821, Palmer came across "strange vessels." He had found an expedition made up of two Russian sloops under the command of Captain Baron Fabian Gottlieb von Bellinghausen. Bellinghausen had been sent by Czar Alexander I "to search for the southern continent."

Later, in describing his brief meeting with the Americans, Bellinghausen told of the young skipper's discovery and referred to the region he found as Palmer's Land. It was through the influence of his Russian rival that the name of Palmer gained a place on the map.

Now known to extend about 700 miles from its base, the region is generally labelled the Palmer Peninsula. Most of the land surface is covered with an immense ice shelf, but under that ice lies a 13,700-foot mountain peak.

Nathaniel Palmer returned to Stonington more excited about the fact that the holds of their ships were bulging with seal skins than about his having reached the last unexplored outpost of our planet. He was master of a vessel that traded in the Spanish Main during 1822-26 and gained regional fame as designer of numerous noted packets and clipper ships. Returning from the Orient, he died in San Francisco on June 21, 1877, still unaware of the importance of the discovery he made at age twenty-one.

America's Greatest Wave of Addiction to "Hard" Drugs Was Triggered by . . . Military Doctors

At the midpoint of the last century, little was known about the long-range effects of narcotics. But opium and its derivatives were effective in easing pain, so "hard" drugs were universally used in military medicine during the Civil War. At war's end, conservative estimates suggest that at least 100,000 veterans—most of whom had fought for the Union—were addicted to opium as a result of battlefield treatment. Total population of the nation was then less than 40,000,000.

Civil War physicians regarded opium as helpful in treatment of dysentery and other common maladies, as well as in relief of intractable pain. So many soldiers used so much of it that civilian demand continued at a high level after hostilities ceased. In 1858 alone, the U.S. imported 71,839 pounds of the powerful narcotic derived from the poppy plant.

The official medicine pannier of the U.S. Army contained fifty-two bottles and vials. None had any marking except an identification number on the top of the cork. Physicians in uniform knew, however, that their basic kit included these drugs:

#14 - cough mixture with opium base
#21 - tincture of opium (often called laudanum)
#28 - paregoric
#33 - opium powder
#39 - morphine sulphate
#40 - pills of opium and camphor
#42 - pills of opium alone

A Confederate medicine wagon carried only twenty drugs in stock. Though prominent on the list, opium and morphine sulphate were often in short supply—hence men in gray ran much less risk of addiction than did their foes in blue.

Used as a painkiller, opium was administered in the form of pills, as a liquid (laudanum), as a camphorated tincture (paregoric), and as morphine. Pills and tinctures were swallowed. Much morphine sulphate was dusted directly into wounds.

At first the hypodermic needle saw little use on the battlefield. Perfected only in 1840, it was not generally familiar to physicians. But as fighting progressed the new instrument came into wider use—almost exclusively for administration of morphine.

In that era, the *U.S. Dispensatory,* or official list of approved drugs, classified opium as "a stimulant narcotic." It was believed to "increase the force, fullness, and frequency of the pulse, augment the temperature of the skin, invigorate the muscular system, quicken the senses, animate the spirits, and give new energy to the intellectual faculties."

Surgeon General Thomas Lawson, who headed the U.S.A. Medical Department at the outbreak of hostilities, had not kept up with the progress of research. He discouraged his officers from purchasing textbooks, doubted the usefulness of the clinical thermometer, and considered the stethoscope "a ridiculous plaything." Small wonder that under Lawson and his successors amputation became the surgical trademark of battlefield medicine.

Forward stations were supposed to be equipped with pails, basins, bandages, splints, and sponges—plus the three great drugs of the era: quinine, chloroform, and opium. Treatment of the wounded was often confined to checking hemorrhage and administering opiates laced with whisky. Most amputations took place in field hospitals, where wounded men received more opium.

Since ancient times it had been known that juice of the poppy, *Papaver somniferum,* relieves many symptoms linked with dysentery. Intestinal disturbances outnumbered all other Civil War maladies, combined. Official medical records of the Union Army list 1,155,266 admissions to sick report for acute diarrhea; 170,488 for chronic diarrhea; 233,812 for acute dysentery; and 25,670 for chronic dysentery.

Conditions in the Army of the Confederacy were even worse. During the first year of fighting, nearly two-thirds of the men in gray were incapacitated for weeks during recurring bouts with dysentery. Confederate medical officer Bedford Brown declared that "nine-tenths of all recruits were attacked by chronic diarrhoea."

In the sick bay as in the surgeon's tent, opium was the great cure-all. Men who had repeated bouts with dysentery, requiring increasingly larger doses with each illness, often became addicted without knowing how the craving was established.

A minority of physicians warned about dangers in promiscuous use of the narcotic. Sanford B. Hunt, M.D., voiced the majority opinion in a report on "Camp Diarrhaea and Dysentery." According to that report, "Opium is the one drug that at least alleviates the alvine flux, even if it does not cure."

Confederate demands for the drug were so great that it played a practically-unknown role in the economics of the Great Rebellion. Early in the conflict, Congress authorized the president to "trade with the Confederacy when it seemed advantageous." In order to keep Billy Yank in the field, the Union urgently needed cotton. In order to keep Johnny Reb in action, the Confederacy had to have opium.

Memphis was the chief center for exchange of Confederate cotton for narcotics plus quinine and chloroform—whose supply was cut off from southern ports by the blockade. In the river city and at other points, North and South exchanged vast quantities of goods with the bargaining power of the drug-rich North rising as the war dragged on.

When hostilities ceased men who had become addicted to opium as a result of medical treatment became confirmed pill takers or "opium eaters." There were no laws governing importation or use of the drug, so the supply remained plentiful.

Many desperate victims tried patent medicines that were advertised as cures. Dr. S. B. Collins, who described himself as "the great narcologist of the age" made a fortune selling his secret but worthless "opium antidote" he claimed to have discovered in 1868.

Some addicts recovered as a result of long and painful effort. Most never mastered the drug. As a result of America's greatest wave of addiction to hard drugs, tens of thousands of Civil War veterans died still hooked upon the narcotics first administered to them through official military channels.

The founder of New Helvetia—the site of present-day Sacramento, California—was Captain John Augustus Sutter. Later he began using his first rather than his middle name.

California Land Baron John A. Sutter Lost a Fortune Instead of Gaining One When Gold Was Found at His Sawmill

A nugget no bigger than a dime started the famous California Gold Rush. It was found on January 24, 1848, by John W. Marshall. Marshall, foreman of a gang of men building a sawmill for land baron John Augustus Sutter, was an ordinary workman but his employer was one of the wealthiest men in the West.

Born in Kandern, Baden, John Sutter came to the U.S. in 1834 at age thirty-one. From St. Louis he crossed the Rockies, then wandered for four years in search of an ideal place to establish a permanent base.

He found it at the site of present-day Sacramento, in a region then held by Mexico. The Swiss emmigrant became a Mexican citizen and received a grant of about 49,000 acres on which he located his settlement of New Helvetia (New Switzerland). Sutter worked so hard to improve transportation and to build villages that he is often called "The Father of California." By the time John Marshall found that all-important nugget, Sutter held what amounted to a private kingdom that was much bigger and richer than the Ponderosa ranch of TV fame.

After the initial find Sutter went with Marshall to the millrace where the sawmill was under construction and himself picked up several tiny nuggets. "I had a signet ring made from them," he later wrote. "I had my father's trademark—a phoenix in flames—engraved on the face. On the inside was the inscription: 'First gold, discovered Jan. 1848.' Three bishop's crosiers followed, then the cross of Basle and my name: SUTTER."

That ring was practically all that John Sutter ever got from the Gold Rush.

Within days after news of Marshall's find had begun spreading, the land baron recorded in his journal: "My workers began to desert. . . . An uninterrupted procession now went past my windows. Everyone who could walk climbed the hills from San Francisco and the coastwise hamlets. As the fever swept the southern towns they too emptied. My poor domain was overrun.

"Misery now began for me. The mills ceased to work. They were plundered to the very mill stones. My tanneries were deserted. My men came to me. They implored me to go to Coloma (about 40 miles north-east of Sutter's Mill), to become a gold-seeker with them. My God! How I loathed it! But I consented at last. There was nothing else for me to do."

"I settled down to wash gold in a mountain camp on the banks of the torrent that is still called Sutter's creek," he recalled in later years. "Soon a horde of adventurers descended upon us. I struck camp and went still higher up the mountain. Useless precaution! That accursed swarm followed us everywhere.

"From the mountain top I could see the immense territory which I had cleared and fertilized given over to fire and pillage. At night the low roar of men on the march came up to us from the west, punctuated by rifle shots. At the end of the bay I watched a vast unknown city arising as though from the ground and spreading visibly each day. The bay was black with vessels."

By October, 1848, one of the interested observers was youthful

Lieutenant William Tecumseh Sherman, destined to win fame as a Civil War general. "People are arriving and departing daily and hourly," he said in a letter sent back east. "At least 400 have come from Oregon already. I have no doubt that gold in these mountains exceeds any previous calculation."

Many of the Argonauts, as gold-seekers were often called, came by wagon train. Others came from the east coast by ship in a matter of about six months. In 1849, more than 700 vessels dropped anchor in San Francisco Bay. Frequently their crews deserted and joined mobs fighting their way to the goldfields.

Inevitably, members of those mobs wrecked and then looted the empire Sutter had created. His buildings were torn down because miners needed lumber to build their shanties. His fine herds of cattle were slaughtered for food. "Shanty towns" made up of board shanties and of tents, sprang up everywhere. Sutter's life was threatened so often that he retreated to isolated Hock Farm, where he remained in virtual hiding for a number of years.

"Johann Augustus Sutter is a ruined man," he confided to his journal. "The watercourses I have made, the sites I chose so carefully for my buildings, the roads I laid out, the bridges and canals that I built are so many baits for the land-grabber and the claim-jumper. New Helvetia? Try to find it! New names are given to everything. Sutterville, Sutter's Creek, Sutter County bear the name of their old master. But these names commemorate nothing save the ruin of my establishment and the tragedy of my fate."

The rush of settlers led to California's admission into the union in 1850. Law was restored, after a fashion. But it was too late for the man who had been forced off a tract of land bigger than the canton of Basle in his native Switzerland. Sutter's domain was now occupied by tens of thousands of adventurers who filed land claims with the U.S. government.

In desperation, John Sutter went to court. Initially he sued the State of California for $25 million and the U.S. government for $50 million damages. Fought for four years, the case went to California's highest court—where Sutter's claims were declared valid. The ruling meant that San Francisco, Sacramento, and dozens of other communities stood on his private property.

News of the legal decision triggered new violence. Mobs attacked and then burned the courthouse where the decision had been rendered. Records of the case went up in smoke. The ranch to which Sutter had retreated was dynamited. His fruit trees were cut down and his cattle were shot.

New litigation brought Sutter a settlement from the State of California: a lifetime annuity of $250 per month. With no resources except that annuity he and his wife Anna took their case to Washington in 1865. California Governor Frederick F. Low, writing on October 6, 1866, said: "I earnestly commend his claims to the favorable consideration of Congress." Mark Twain, General James W. Denver, and other nationally prominent men came to Sutter's support. But "A Bill for the Relief of John A. Sutter" died in a Senate committee.

Living in a cheap boarding house, Sutter stayed in the capital in order to press his claims. April 15, 1876, saw Congress receive a sixteen-page memorial signed by General Sherman and several hundred prominent Californians. The Private Land Claims Committee of the House of Representatives recommended passage of a bill granting redress to Sutter. But this bill, and numerous later ones, failed.

On May 12, 1879, the San Francisco *Daily Alta California* ran a special editorial. Sutter was praised for opening up California, and readers were given a capsule account of his long struggle. Editors damned shysters and land grabbers who had seized his holdings, and urged Congressional action.

By then, John Augustus Sutter was past caring. Feeble and stone broke, he was in a state of deep depression.

A new bill for relief of Sutter was reported favorably by a House committee on April 8, 1880. Before the bill reached the floor of the lawmaking body the man driven from his empire by gold-seekers died a pauper, on June 18, 1880.

Sutter's Fort as it appeared in 1930

Orville Wright was at the controls for the 12-second first flight of an airplane at Kitty Hawk, N.C., December 17, 1903. He flew about 100 feet; later the same day, Wilbur covered 852 feet in 59 seconds

An Ohio Farm Boy Contracted a Lifelong Case of "Airplane Fever" While Recuperating from Typhoid

Late in July, 1896, Orville Wright came down with a fever. The family doctor examined him and pronounced it to be "a routine case of typhoid fever." Medically speaking, the diagnosis was correct. But from other perspectives it was the most mistaken diagnosis of the century—for the patient contracted "airplane fever" while recuperating.

    Just fifteen years old when he became ill, Orville was already keenly interested in "nearly anything dealing with science." Like typical typhoid victims of the era, he fought for his life a few days. After his delirium passed, he remained housebound for weeks. It was during that period of enforced idleness that he and his brother Wilbur became enamored with the goal of manned flight.

Younger of five children born to Milton and Susan Wright, Wilbur and Orville very early learned to rely largely on their own resources. Their mother died while they were young. Their father, a bishop in the United Brethren Church, was often away from home for extended periods.

Lorin and Reuchlin, the two older children, had already married and left home. That meant that Katherine, the only girl in the family, had to assume the role of mother to her younger brothers. "Katherine was home from Oberlin College, on summer vacation, when I took typhoid," Orville recalled. "A trained nurse came in to help look after me when I was out of my head, but Katherine and Wilbur were my real nurses."

Each boy had his own room—just wide enough to hold a single bed plus a wash-stand and a chair. They didn't find the four years' difference in their age a barrier; almost from the time they learned to read, they read aloud to one another.

"Since I continued to be very weak even after getting over the worst of the fever, it was Wilbur who did all the reading that summer and most of the fall," Orville said. "Wilbur brought home a newspaper one day. He showed me a headline and exclaimed: 'Otto Lilienthal is dead!' "

A few months earlier, the science-oriented boys had learned a little about the noted German engineer. They knew that he had spent years studying the flight of birds, and from that study had learned how to design gliders that sometimes made wind-borne flights of considerable distance. It was on such a flight that the pioneer aeronautical engineer was killed.

Lilienthal, the Wright brothers learned from the news account of his death, was reputed to have had "more flying practice than any man alive." Yet dozens of successful flights during a period of more than five years had kept him airborne for a total of less than five hours.

Orville and Wilbur Wright talked after the older brother had finished reading the account of the accident that took Lilienthal's life. Then they fell silent for a time. Lying flat on his back in his sickbed, Orville resumed the conversation by posing a question. With the great pioneer of flight dead, who would take up his work and build—not a glider, but a flying machine?

Orville Wright at age 8; his brother, Wilbur (right) at age 13

Solemnly, the two boys concluded that they would do the job! Their decision was reached seriously, not lightly. They knew that many persons had tried to develop machines that would bear humans into the air, and that all had failed. But with "lots of time" on his hands as he recuperated, Orville believed he could use that time to find out what others had done, and perhaps devise a new approach to the problem.

When Katherine went back to college at the beginning of the fall term her youngest brother was still unable to leave the house. All that momentous fall, Wilbur read to Orville everything he could find in the Dayton Public Library about aviation. When local resources had been exhausted, the adolescents wrote to the Smithsonian Institution and asked for material about flying. They didn't then dream that they were destined to compete with Smithsonian executive Samuel Langley for the honor of being first to get an engine-powered craft into the air.

Though self-taught, the brothers were already skilled craftsmen. When they opened a bicycle shop they didn't stop with selling bikes, but learned to make all sorts of repairs and innovations. Their first biplane kite, built in August, 1899, included parts from dismembered

Bicycle shop of the Wright Brothers, behind which was the shed where they built the engine for their 1903 plane

bicycles. When Orville became the first man in history to guide a plane off the ground, the one-time invalid sat at the controls of the *Flyer*—named for bicycles he and his brother had handled back in Dayton.

After they had gained world fame, the brothers indicated in numerous interviews and talks that they never really considered whether or not they would devote their lives to science. They took that for granted from childhood. Looking back, however, they realized that they were interested in so many aspects of science that they were in danger of concentrating upon none.

It was news of the death of a noted German glider pilot, brought into a sickroom, that led the brothers to discard "a multitude of interests" and to concentrate on a single grand goal—conquest of the skies by means of powered flight. Because Wilbur outlived his brother by 36 years, he is the more widely known of the pair. But it was Orville, victim of "flying fever contracted while recuperating from typhoid fever," who was at the controls of the *Flyer* when the machine took off under its own power in December, 1903, for a maiden flight of twelve seconds and a distance of about 100 feet.

Spanish warships in Pensacola Bay

Britain's American Foster-Colony Was Snatched by Spanish

If you can name all 13 of Britain's New World Colonies that rebelled and won, your memory is good. But even teachers are seldom able to name her American colonies that did not rebel.

Three foster-colonies, originally settled by the French and the Spanish, are usually overlooked. They changed hands when the Treaty of Paris was signed in 1763. In Europe it ended the Seven Years War; in North America it brought the French and Indian War to a close.

Because Britain was the big winner in the struggle with France and Spain, she got lots of land in the settlement: Canada, East Florida, and West Florida. That brought her North American colonies to 16.

WEST FLORIDA — THE SIXTEENTH COLONY

West Florida stretched from Pensacola to the Mississippi River. East Florida, with government centered in St. Augustine, was more highly developed. Together, the two Floridas were valued less highly than some island posts. England had captured Cuba during the years of fighting; when peace came she grudgingly swapped the island for the Floridas.

Modern-day strategists would rejoice at such an arrangement. With boundaries of her colonies settled by Englishmen now extended to the Mississippi River, Britain had a firm grasp upon an entire continent.

Her traders were astute enough to take advantage of the situation. Pensacola, permanently colonized by the Spanish in 1698, became a hub of commercial activity. British-made trinkets plus rum, blankets, and kettles were swapped for furs and other commodities brought by Indians.

Commercial ties became so strong that when the American Revolution broke out Britain could and did rely heavily upon Indian allies.

Britain's policy-makers, far removed from the scene of action, didn't have the viewpoint or zeal of her overseas merchants and speculators. King George III, subject to attacks of mental illness that began in 1765, had little interest in the Americas.

Spanish troops advance by land

Lord George Germain, Britain's Secretary of State for the Colonies, never set foot upon American soil. That gave British commanders in the field virtually complete responsibility for major policy decisions as well as for conduct of the war.

Sir Henry Clinton, a veteran professional soldier, succeeded Sir William Howe as commander in chief in North America in 1778. He was sufficiently aware of the strategic importance of the South to recapture Georgia and to commit large numbers of troops to the Carolinas. Yet he showed no interest at all in the Floridas.

Failure to strengthen garrisons there may have stemmed from the fact that neither of these colonies showed the least inclination to join in the Revolution.

Unlike England's ruler, Spain's King Carlos III was intensely interested in the New World. He held most of South America, but was keenly conscious of having lost most North American holdings. A great-grandson of King Louis XIV of France, it was natural for Carlos to join France in supporting insurgent English colonists overseas.

Carlos was not interested in these colonists—but he had a deep-seated hatred of England. Anything that hurt England was good for Spain, he reasoned. In 1762, just three years after assuming the throne, he joined France (also England's foe) in the secret Treaty of Fountainbleau. By that treaty, Spain got all of Louisiana west of the Mississippi River.

Britain's failure to win a quick victory over Americans who had rebelled made her enemies bold. Spain declared war upon the island empire in 1779 and moved against her in the Old World and the New.

Besieged by the Spanish, Gibraltar proved too tough to be taken quickly: there the struggle dragged on for years.

It was a different story overseas. Youthful Bernardo de Galvez, Governor of Louisiana, moved swiftly and forcefully against the British. He captured Mobile in 1780, then proceeded to strengthen it as a Spanish foothold in West Florida. Galvez saw the region as crucial in the contest for a continent.

Early in 1781 he assembled 64 ships and 4,000 men in Havana. They entered Pensacola Bay on March 8. Though the British commander of Ft. George tried his best to hold the vital fortress, his resources were limited. Arrival of an additional 1,000 Spanish troops in late March spelled the beginning of the end.

Two hundred years ago, on May 9, 1781, Pensacola surrendered

Sir Henry Clinton, top British commander in the New World

to the Spanish. Few present-day Americans ever heard of the battle. Yet historian N. Orwin Rush regards it as perhaps the most important one of the Revolutionary era. By the loss of her 16th colony that commanded much of the Gulf, Britain forfeited an opportunity to put victorious American rebels between pincers: Canada on the north and West Florida on the south.

Sick of the whole North American enterprise, just two years after the fall of Pensacola Britain swapped East Florida to Spain for the Bahamas.

How the two Floridas became part of the United States is another story. Had Pensacola been strengthened sufficiently to withstand Spanish attack, it's within the realm of possibility that the entire southeastern tip of North America would still be British.

West front of Jefferson's mansion, circa 1782

Old and Broke, Thomas Jefferson Tried (But Failed) to Pay His Debts by Selling His Plantation at Lottery

In January, 1826, eighty-three-year-old Thomas Jefferson wrote to his grandson that he did not have enough cash on hand to meet obligations due local merchants for household items. Other desperate measures designed to recoup his fortunes had failed. So the ex-president persuaded the Virginia legislature to let him offer most of his land in a lottery. In spite of his great prestige, the lottery got little support—so little that when the ex-president died on Independence Day he left his family a mountain of debts.

For many years, Jefferson had owned thousands of acres of land. In 1782 only one man in Albermarle County, Virginia, owned more slaves than did Jefferson. But for most of his adult life he showed a knack for spending money faster than he made it. During his last full year as president, 1808, his out-go was almost $750 a month more than his combined income as chief executive and owner of a vast plantation.

At the end of his term as president, the founding father owned at least $8,000 on his own signature—and was obligated to pay another promissory note that he had persuaded James Madison to endorse so he could get much-needed cash.

In spite of his bleak financial outlook, the man who had drafted the Declaration of Independence never learned to restrain his spending. Captain Edmund Bacon, long-time overseer at Monticello, said that "many weeks, the twenty-six spare horse stalls were not sufficient to accommodate the mounts of visitors. I have often sent a wagon-load of hay up to the stable, and the next morning there would not be enough to make a bird's nest."

Monticello was always open to Jefferson's host of friends. Sometimes several dozen were on hand simultaneously; some stayed for weeks. Cost of playing the open-handed host drove Jefferson deeper into debt. So did his liking for fine horses and fancy rigs.

Matters became so bad that the scholarly Virginia gentleman reluctantly decided to part with one of his most prized possessions—his fine library. It was needed in Washington, where the Library of Congress had gone up in smoke during 1814 attacks upon the capital by British forces.

After the British withdrew, Thomas Jefferson wrote to his old friend Samuel Harrison Smith and authorized him to offer the Jefferson library to Congress—for a price. "I have been fifty years making it," Jefferson wrote. He did not have an exact catalogue, but was positive that it included more than 6,000 volumes—"all of them fine ones, selected with care."

Several key Congressional leaders of the era were long-time political foes of Jefferson, and were not eager to give him aid. In spite of their opposition, the lawmaking body eventually voted to accept the offer of the former president and to pay him $23,950 for books that became the nucleus of today's Library of Congress.

Even this money was not nearly enough to get Jefferson out of trouble with his creditors. As debts mounted, he continued to expand and to improve Monticello and to entertain lavishly. Eventually his unpaid obligations reached a total of more than $107,000—a staggering sum for the era.

Hoping to recoup his finances, he lay awake at night wondering what assets he could liquidate. In January, 1826, he sent his grandson Jefferson Randolph to Richmond on an urgent mission. "I have a scheme for a lottery," he confided to a few intimates. "It will injure no one, but to me it is almost a question of life and death."

In order to implement his plan, he needed a bill of authorization from the state legislature. Supporting his proposal, Thomas Jefferson wrote: "It is a common idea that games of chance are immoral. But what is chance? If we consider chance immoral, then every pursuit of human industry is immoral."

His personal dilemma, he confided in a February 17 letter to James Madison, "stemmed largely from the fact that property (land) has lost its character of being a resource. So the idea occurred to me of selling by way of lottery."

Many Virginia legislators were wary of the proposal. Jefferson's old friend, Joseph Cabell, served as a one-man lobby to work for support of a favorable bill. He recruited Dabney Carr, Jr., to assist him but the two received little encouragement. Young Jefferson Randolph ruefully reported to his grandfather that "The policy of this state has been against lotteries as immoral, and the first view of the subject was calculated to give alarm."

A few supporters of Jefferson tried to generate interest in providing from the state an $80,000 loan that would be interest-free for his life. This plan ended in talk. Finally the lower house of the legislature passed the Jefferson Lottery Bill by a margin of just four votes. In the senate, resistance collapsed a few days later.

Elaborate plans were made, and a sales organization was estab-

Still well preserved during the 1830s, Monticello was locally recognized as "America's finest private residence" (steel engraving from Dix watercolor)

Ticket for unsuccessful Jefferson lottery by which the ex-president proposed to place his finances in liquid state

lished with branches in big cities outside Virginia as well as throughout the state. Even though Virginia Governor John Tyler lent his personal prestige to sales rallies, the response was poor.

Two of Jefferson's old political rivals—John Randolph and John Marshall—surprised everyone by buying batches of lottery tickets. "Out of pity that the author of the Declaration of Independence has suffered public humiliation," John Randolph alone bought $500 worth of tickets.

In spite of such support, it was soon clear that the lottery would not produce enough money to pay the debts of Thomas Jefferson. Eventually the plan was abandoned. As a substitute for the lottery, without Jefferson's knowledge his friends opened "public subscriptions" for his financial relief. New Yorkers alone sent $8,500. $5,000 came from Philadelphia, $3,000 from Baltimore, and smaller sums from other cities.

Yet all efforts had failed to produce even half of the $107,000 that Jefferson owed. At his death on July 4, 1826, the third President of the U.S. left so many unpaid obligations that executors eventually sold his beloved Monticello at auction. Before the mansion became recognized as a major national shrine, nearly a century later, it had fallen into disrepair. Great care has been taken in restoring it to condition and furnishings as nearly as possible like those in the era when Jefferson ran up debts by holding open house all year around.

Today the land that Jefferson couldn't move even by means of a lottery is so valuable that a few choice acres at current prices would retire $107,000 in debts and leave a credit balance.

Commemorative postage stamp portrays a daintily feminine medal wearer

First Female Medic Got Congressional Medal of Honor

Volunteer service with the 52nd Ohio Infantry during the fall of 1863 led to thè first—and only—award of a Congressional Medal of Honor to a female. Mary Walker, M.D., got it for conspicuous bravery in aiding wounded men in blue . . . while concurrently doing all she could to alleviate the suffering of rebel civilians.

Born in Oswego, New York, in 1832, she studied medicine in spite of the fact that folk of the era looked with scandalized disapproval upon the idea of a woman doctor. She got her certificate from Syracuse Medical College in 1855. Attempts to establish a practice in

Columbus, Ohio, and in Rome, New York, met downright opposition because of her sex.

That's one reason she seized upon the Civil War as a chance to serve the Union. As an army medic—working unofficially without pay in a prototype of a modern MASH unit—she defied tradition by wearing trousers. But when possible she kept her hair in curls so she'd be recognized as a female.

After a series of rebuffs from military brass she left Washington late in the summer of 1863 and headed for the Tennessee front. All observers saw a major battle in the making there. General W. S. Rosencrans' Federal Army of the Cumberland had already crossed the

Artist's sketch portrays somewhat masculine-looking Dr. Mary Walker

Medic's tent, Army of the Cumberland

Tennessee River and had Chattanooga as a target. General Braxton Bragg's Confederate Army of Tennessee had reluctantly abandoned the city and had withdrawn into north Georgia.

After days of reconnaissance and skirmishing, enemy forces gradually took up battle stations. They moved slowly, for both commanders realized that their meeting could be decisive. A Union victory would put Atlanta and all Georgia in jeopardy; a Confederate victory would end what seemed the best chance to cut the Confederacy in half. September 19th and 20th saw 58,000 Federal and 66,000 Confederate troops meet in one of the bloodiest conflicts of the war: the Battle of Chickamauga.

Late on the afternoon of the 20th, Confederate General James Longstreet broke through a gap in enemy lines and was within a hair's breadth of a smashing victory. But Federal General George H. Thomas, holding Snodgrass Hill, repelled one wave of assault after another. His stand prevented wholesale panic among Union forces and earned him the nickname "Rock of Chickamauga." With two-thirds of the Union army, Thomas fell back to Rossville, Ga.

So the Atlanta *Intelligencer* was less than accurate in an exultant account that ended with the claim: "The enemy no longer pollutes Georgia soil . . ." At enormous sacrifice rebels actually had won a tactical victory. Both sides suffered 28% casualties: 18,454 Confederate and 16,170 Union.

It was wounded men in blue to whom Dr. Mary Walker hoped to minister. Somehow she managed to get the ear of General Thomas. He gave his approval to her appointment as assistant surgeon of the 52nd Ohio Infantry, replacing an officer who had died suddenly. Regimental commander Colonel Dan McCook was so desperate for medical help that he welcomed the woman into his unit.

Enlisted men viewed matters differently. They wanted no part of a female doctor in trousers. According to regimental historian the Reverend Nixon B. Steward, the men seemed almost to hate the woman who tried to alleviate their suffering.

While still on active duty with the 52nd Ohio, Dr. Mary Walker began roaming about the Tennessee-Georgia hill country in order to minister to Confederate civilians. She found entire families in which all the males, including the 16-year-olds, had gone off to war. Women and children often hid in thickets and swamps. Many were in dire need of medical aid. So the Yankee doctor borrowed freely from army stores to help the destitute sick.

While on an errand of mercy in April, 1864, Mary Walker was captured and delivered to General D. H. Hill as a prisoner of war. After a brief stay in Dalton, Ga., she was shipped to Richmond, Va., and confined in Castle Thunder. Exchanged along with several hundred other prisoners, she was taken back inside Union lines in August, 1864. Two months later she won a contract as Acting Assistant Surgeon, U. S. Army. That made her the first female to serve in such capacity in official U. S. military annals. Immediately she got permission to join Sherman's forces—but missed connections because the March to the Sea had already started.

An executive order was signed, but before Mary Walker got the award Lincoln intended for her, the president was shot. Years later, on January 24, 1886, intentions of the martyred president were carried out: Mary Walker became the first (and only) woman to receive the Congressional Medal of Honor. Generals Thomas and Sherman had initiated the award, citing her valuable service to the government in the aftermath of Chickamauga.

Dr. Walker seldom appeared in public without her medal. Then in 1917 a special review board disqualified 911 awards—including hers. She defied Congress and refused to return the medal or to cease wearing it. Still proudly displaying the controversial bronze conferred for action in Tennessee and Georgia, 88-year-old Mary Walker fell on the steps of the Capitol and died.

Another "first and only" came long afterward. Acting on the recommendation of the Army Board for the Correction of Military Records, in 1977 Army Secretary Clifford Alexander posthumously restored Dr. Mary Walker's medal that was originally conferred upon authorization of Abraham Lincoln. That made her the only person ever to be awarded the Congressional Medal of Honor twice.

By the time of that belated second award, male military and political leaders were moving toward understanding what Dr. Mary Walker could have told them long ago: that females—when given the opportunity—can and will perform even on the battlefield as well as males—and sometimes better.

Millions saw her picture for the first time when she was honored by a commemorative postage stamp. As depicted on that stamp, she is dainty and feminine—but proud to display the only Congressional Medal of Honor ever conferred upon a female.

Steamer PHILADELPHIA, sister-ship to the ill-fated PENNSYLVANIA, and virtually identical in construction

Mark Twain's Hot Temper Cost Him His Berth on a Mississippi River Steamer—and Saved His Life

Samuel L. Clemens, destined to gain lasting fame under the pen name of Mark Twain, very early established a high goal for himself. He wanted to spend his life on the Mississippi River—in the well-paid post of pilot. Before getting that all-important license in April, 1859, he went through a long period of training.

Much of his apprenticeship was spent working as a steersman. That's the post he held on the steamer *Pennsylvania,* twin vessel to the *Philadelphia,* during most of 1858. Because Twain's hot temper flared and he quarreled with his pilot, he was put off the vessel in New

Orleans. Loss of his berth saved his life—for otherwise he would have been aboard when the *Pennsylvania* exploded and burned on June 13, 1858.

Born in the village of Florida, Missouri, in 1835, Sam Clemens moved with his family to Hannibal in 1839. He was a frail and sickly child who walked in his sleep and often ran away from home. At eighteen he left home for good in order to go to St. Louis and hunt a job. Already, he yearned to become a riverboat pilot.

Jobs proved scarce in St. Louis, so Sam set out for New York to see the Crystal Palace exhibition. That trip was the beginning of a two-year period of wandering during which he worked at odd jobs. After spending the winter of 1856 in Cincinnati he managed to get passage to New Orleans, with the idea of using that port as a jumping-off place for South America.

Horace Bixby, pilot of the steamer *Paul Jones* on which Sam travelled from Cincinnati to New Orleans, became fond of his passenger. Instead of going to South America, Bixby argued, the youth should work toward his dream of becoming a licensed river pilot. Once he got that license, he could earn $150 to $250 a month—and enjoy a position of prestige.

Clemens quickly accepted the chance to become an apprentice, responsible during training to his pilot. Up and down the river he become known as "one of Horace Bixby's cubs." Bixby, in turn, was promised a total of $500 for teaching the pilot's trade to Clemens.

By 1858 Sam had become a competent steersman. Already he had memorized many details of the approximately 1200-mile stretch of river between New Orleans and St. Louis. Still making installment payments to Bixby, he was transferred by ship owners to the sidewheeler *Pennsylvania*—and placed under the jurisdiction of her pilot.

In his famous *Life on the Mississippi,* Twain gave a vivid description of the pilot of the *Pennsylvania,* invariably designated simply as "Mr. Brown."

"He was a middle-aged, long, slim, bony, smooth-shaven, horse-faced, ignorant, stingy, malicious, snarling, fault-finding, mote-magnifying tyrant," according to Twain. "I early got the habit of coming on watch with dread in my heart. No matter how good a time I might have been having with the off-watch below, and no matter how high my spirits might be when I started aloft, my soul became lead in my body when I approached the pilot-house."

During several months that 'Horace Bixby's cub' worked as steersman under Mr. Brown, the two developed increasing mutual animosity. "The moment I was in Mr. Brown's presence, even in the darkest night, I could feel those yellow eyes upon me, and knew their owner was watching for a pretext to spit out some venom on me," Twain later wrote.

"I often wanted to kill Brown, but this would not answer. A cub had to take everything his boss gave; and we all believed that there was a United States law making it a penitentiary offense to strike or threaten a pilot who was on duty.

"However, I could *imagine* myself killing Brown; there was no law against that; and that was the thing I used always to do the moment I was abed. Instead of going over my river in my mind, as was my duty, I threw business aside for pleasure and killed Brown. I killed Brown every night for months; not in old, stale, commonplace ways, but in new and picturesque ones."

Sam Clemens managed to keep his anger bottled up inside himself until his superior officer made a savage attack upon Henry, his younger brother who had joined the ship's crew as a common laborer. After giving Henry Clemens a tongue-lashing, Brown picked up a ten-pound lump of coal and started to hit him.

"I was between," said Mark Twain, "with a heavy stool, and I hit Brown a good honest blow which stretched him out. I had committed the crime of crimes—I had lifted my hand against a pilot on duty! I supposed I was booked for the penitentiary, sure."

Though he hadn't committed a criminal offense, the youthful steersman really was in serious trouble. Brown might well prevent him from ever getting his pilot's license. That issue would have to be resolved in the future; for the moment, Brown merely ordered his subordinate out of the pilot-house and told him never to come back. Then he sent for Captain Klinefelter, master of the vessel, and demanded that Clemens be put off the ship.

In New Orleans, Klinefelter—threatened with the loss of his pilot—capitulated. He ordered Sam to "tend wharf" for a few days, then to join the crew of another vessel scheduled to follow the *Pennsylvania* upstream.

Sam Clemens protested and threatened—and then gave up his berth. He supervised loading cotton and other commodities and after 48 hours climbed aboard the *A. T. Lacey* for the voyage to St. Louis.

Samuel Clemens (Mark Twain) won coveted "Pilot's Certificate" in April, 1859

When the vessel reached Greenville, Mississippi, crewmen heard the dreadful news: boilers of the *Pennsylvania* had blown up on June 13, 1858, when the steamer was about four hours below Memphis.

Mr. Brown no longer posed a threat to the steersman who wanted to become a pilot; he was dead. So was Henry Clemens. So were Captain Klinefelter and 157 others aboard the ill-fated vessel.

Though it is little known to modern Americans, the explosion of the *Pennsylvania* ranks among the worst of all disasters to sidewheeler steamers. So few passengers and members of the crew survived that had steersman Sam Clemens been aboard he almost certainly would have perished. His hot temper that led him to strike his pilot saved his life and made it possible for Mark Twain to give Tom Sawyer and Huck Finn to the world.

James Waddell, skipper of the Shenandoah, *was an Annapolis graduate*

Last Cruise of Raider *Shenandoah* Was Her Most Deadly

Robert E. Lee's surrender of the Army of Northern Virginia on April 9, 1865, officially ended the Civil War. But because the commanding officer of a Confederate warship didn't get the news, he continued to lead his crew against Union vessels for months. When he finally learned that the Confederacy had capitulated, James I. Waddell took the C.S.S. *Shenandoah* to England in order to give her up.

Small by today's standards, the vessel logged 58,000 miles on her last voyage. During the last 6 months of it (after Lee's surrender) the 227-foot raider captured at least 38 Union merchant ships. Thirty-two of them, valued empty at $1,172,223, were burned or scuttled. Concurrently, 1,053 prisoners were taken—without a single casualty on either side—in a running sea battle that girdled the globe.

Early in the war veteran shipping expert James D. Bulloch was made a special agent representing the Southern cause. Since shipbuilding activity had been concentrated in the North, Confederates lacked skill to build their own warships. Bulloch reached Liverpool, England, on June 4, 1861, and began a shrewd program of undercover purchasing that eventually gave the Confederacy a fledgling navy. Only one vessel in that navy, the *Shenandoah,* ever circumnavigated the globe.

When launched in Britain the vessel was called the *Sea King*. As a merchantman she made at least one trip to India. Bulloch bought the unarmed ship and on October 8, 1864, managed to get her out of British waters. To avoid violating Britain's neutrality she left port accompanied by the tender *Laurel*—which carried a full load of guns and ammunition destined to be transferred to the *Sea King*.

At Funchal, Madeira, guns and ammunition went aboard the larger vessel. Renamed the *Shenandoah,* she was commissioned a vessel of the Navy of the Confederate States of America. Problems erupted at once. When members of the English crew learned what was afoot 42 demanded to be put ashore at Tenerife, leaving only 20 men aboard.

Waddell used persuasion plus offers of bounty to recruit more crewmen from ships captured by the *Shenandoah*; eventually he had 51 men and 22 officers under his command. Some natives of New England—plus a few free blacks—willingly fought under him.

A fully rigged sailing vessel equipped with auxiliary steam power, the raider crossed the Atlantic. Then Waddell headed for Australia by way of the Cape of Good Hope. Australia, he reasoned, would be an ideal jumping-off place from which to move against Yankee whalers. Sure enough, he found 4 of them in the Caroline Islands and captured them without a fight.

With her prizes in her wake the *Shenandoah* reached Ascension Island on April 1, 1865. Unaware that Lee was about to capitulate to Grant, Captain Waddell burned the captured whalers while peace negotiations were getting under way in far-off Virginia. A month later, having no idea that the war was over, Waddell put 130 prisoners ashore and headed for the Arctic Circle. There the Confederate raider found the prey she was seeking.

In an awesome 7-day period (June 22–28, 1865) the sleek warship captured 24 ships belonging to the "enemy" merchant fleet. All but 4 were burned. Ships that were saved were used as cartels with which to transport hundreds of prisoners. With the 14 other vessels taken by the *Shenandoah* on her last cruise total damage inflicted ran to a total of $6,488,320.

Newspapers found aboard a captured ship reported Lee's surrender. But the same papers carried a story with a Danville, Va. dateline which said Jefferson Davis had issued a proclamation urging loyal Confederates to fight harder than ever. Waddell had heard that San Francisco was defended by just one Union ironclad. It would be a great feather in his own cap and a boost to Confederate morale, he reasoned, to destroy that ship as a prelude to capturing San Francisco and demanding a heavy ransom.

With this goal in mind Waddell directed his raider down the western coast of North America. On August 2, 1865, he sighted the British-operated *Baracouta*. He hailed the ship and asked for news of the war. "What war?" demanded the English skipper.

Finally convinced that the North/South struggle was over Waddell told his men that they would seek sanctuary in British waters. But instead of heading for Australia, he charted a dangerous 17,000-mile course whose destination was Liverpool. Literally a ship without a country, the *Shenandoah* sailed for more than 3 months toward her final destination.

Big, handsome James Waddell, age 41, brought his raider into St. George's Channel on November 5. There he picked up a pilot who guided the warship up the Mersey river to Liverpool. Limping from a wound sustained in a duel, the last Confederate officer to give up the fight formally surrendered his vessel to British authorities on November 6th.

By then leaders of the island kingdom knew that the United States would seek compensation for damage done by the *Shenandoah* and other British-built vessels. So it was announced that any United States or British citizen aboard the surrendered raider would be put under arrest. Not a man in the entire crew admitted allegiance to either country; those who didn't call themselves citizens of the Confederate States of America listed European, Asiatic, or Pacific Island citizenship.

Turned over to United States authorities, the ship from whose decks the last gun of the Civil War was fired was sold at auction — to

At anchor in a British port, the Shenandoah *was a ship without a country*

the Sultan of Zanzibar. She perished during a storm in the Indian Ocean in 1879.

James Waddell remained in Europe for a few years, then returned home and became a captain in the service of the U. S. Pacific Mail Co. He spent his last years in Annapolis, Md., because he had especially fond memories of his years there as a cadet in the U. S. Naval Academy.

Waddell died in Annapolis on March 15, 1886. Few men in the annals of the sea could match his accomplishments. But opposite his name in the records of the U. S. Navy there is no list of ships captured — simply the one-word entry: "Dismissed."

Notes Scribbled on an Envelope by Self-Taught Musician Daniel Butterfield Brought Him the Only Lasting Niche He Won

Daniel Butterfield, born on October 31, 1831, in Utica, New York, was a true 19th-century American "man of all parts." He rose through the ranks to the post of major general in the U.S. Army. He built a railroad in Guatemala, later tried without success to get permission to build a trans-Siberian railroad. President of the Albany & Troy Steamboat Co., owner of the Brooklyn Annex steamships, and director of Mechanics & Traders Bank of New York, it was Butterfield whom the U.S. Postmaster General picked to study postal systems of London and Paris in 1870 in order to bring home ideas. Military forces throughout the world use the shoulder patch he originated to identify men of his Civil War unit.

Yet the versatile administrator, originator, and successful money-maker would be all but forgotten today had he not felt that he could improve on the bugle call "Extinguish Lights" that had long been the traditional final signal of the military day. At a low point in the morale of Union forces, in July, 1862, Butterfield was struck by what he considered to be the "musical pomposity" of the long-established bugle call.

"That signal is entirely too formal," he observed. "Men who are risking their lives in the name of freedom are sent to their cots by notes that resemble a trumpeting welcome to a foreign potentate. They should go to their slumber inspired to sleep well and hope for the coming of a better dawn."

To back up his verdict about "Extinguish Lights," the brigadier general whose troops had covered withdrawal of the Army of the Potomac to Harrison's Landing, Virginia, pulled an envelope from his pocket and quickly scribbled notes across its back. Next day he instructed brigade bugler Oliver W. Norton, of the 83rd Pennsylvania Infantry, to play the hastily-improvised call. Butterfield made a few minor changes in it, then ordered that in his brigade it should be substituted for "Extinguish Lights."

Soldiers who first heard the combination of notes said they were impressed as well as inspired. Few fighting forces of modern times have been in greater need of inspiration. Stonewall Jackson's men had humiliated Union leaders in the Shenandoah Valley. Robert E. Lee had taken the offensive against McClelland and was pushing his men away from the Confederate capital that only weeks earlier had seemed a plum ripe for the plucking. Civilian leaders in the north were already becoming weary of the war, and now it was clear that there could be no swift, easy victory.

There are many traditions about how Daniel Butterfield's new bugle call came to be known as "Taps." No such story can be documented. But abundant evidence—mostly from letters and informal diaries of fighting men—supports the verdict that "Taps" surged to popularity more rapidly than any other unpublished musical composition in history.

By the time the composer had been given command of the 5th Army Corps, on November 16, 1862, his bugle call had been adopted by one or more units in each of the Union armies. Before Christmas it was in universal use by blue-clad buglers—and in one of the strangest developments in a war filled with contradictions and paradoxes, it was by then semi-official among men in gray as well for proximity of fighting forces had enabled Confederate officers to hear the new call. Hearing it, many liked it so well that they ordered their own buglers to use it as the last signal of the day.

Many who heard and liked the hasty composition of the amateur musician didn't fully agree with his judgment about its effects. Perhaps it was intended to inspire hope for the coming dawn, but there was a peculiarly poignant—indeed, a unique—quality of what some called "muted sorrow" in the combination of bugle notes. This factor clearly fostered the quick rise and rapid spread of using the new melody for a man's "last call" as he was lowered into his grave.

Daniel Butterfield himself, by then a retired major general, experienced the special impact of "Taps" in 1888. That year, a quarter-century after the battle of Gettysburg (in which the composer of "Taps" was severely wounded), veterans of the bloody conflict gathered for a reunion. At first it seemed that survivors of those three bloody days would rear new walls of hostility between North and South.

Late in the day on July 2, as dusk approached, a bugler scrambled to a position on Little Round Top hill. From that height he played "Taps" and the notes of the universally-known melody fell on men camped along Cemetery Ridge and Seminary Ridge. Butterfield's personal reaction echoed that of multitudes of former enemies. "In a way I cannot explain," he wrote, "that bugle call by a soldier whose name I never learned wiped from my memory the last trace of bitterness carried over from the battlefields. When I reached Little Round Top I saw no blue or gray uniforms—just old comrades."

Most business exploits of the composer took place in postwar years. Successful in nearly everything he undertook, he experienced just one personal disaster. As assistant U.S. treasurer in the Grant administration he was stationed in New York—where he became entangled in the Jay Gould manipulations of the gold market that led to Black Friday, a notorious 1869 day of calamity for Wall Street and for U.S. business. Butterfield (who realized substantial profits from his ties with Gould) always maintained that he was naive rather than crooked, and the verdict of history supports his claim.

At his death in 1901 it was not the successful international businessman or even the veteran of Chancellorsville, Gettysburg, Lookout Mountain and Sherman's march to the sea . . . but the composer of "Taps" who became one of the few non-graduates to be buried at West Point.

Van Buren (center) is depicted as having had a nightmare because of a cider barrel (Harrison's symbol)

A Request for $3,655 Helped to Defeat Martin Van Buren in His Bid for Another Term in the White House

Today, the cost of a presidential campaign by a major political party runs into many millions of dollars. But in 1840 foes made political hay out of just $3,665. A major factor leading to Martin Van Buren's defeat in his bid for reelection was "extravagance" symbolized by a request that now would be considered trivial.

At the president's request, friends on Capitol Hill tacked a $3,665 amendment to a bill expected to win quick approval. Under terms of the amendment, that sum would be made available for improvements in the White House.

101

Whig Representative Charles Ogle of Somerset, Pa., saw an opportunity in the request. Speaking in the House of Representatives on April 14, 1840, he attacked the occupant of the White House as "financially irresponsible."

Ogle's carefully prepared attack was a mixture of truth, exaggeration, and outright falsehoods. But Whigs made it *the* campaign document of the 1840 contest. It exploded with such violence that though Van Buren won unanimous renomination from the Democrats, he carried just 7 out of the 26 states.

One of the few incumbent presidents who lost a reelection bid, Van Buren was the son of a New York farmer and innkeeper. He was reared in a lower middle class family. The first president to be born a United States citizen, he hitched his political wagon to the star of Andrew Jackson. In the election of 1836 he received 762,678 popular votes against 735,561 for Whig candidate William Henry Harrison.

Van Buren took the oath of office on March 4, 1837. He offended many voters by riding to the inauguration ceremony in an elegant phaeton complete with liveried servants. The vehicle was built from wood obtained from the famous frigate, the *Constitution.*

New York was emerging as a major urban center, with Philadelphia and Baltimore beginning to be sophisticated. As a whole, though, America was still rural—oriented toward hard manual labor and strict frugality.

Pigs and chickens roamed about the streets of Washington at will. Many streets were criss-crossed with cowpaths and open ditches. Charles Dickens visited the nation's capital during this era and found it "unbelievably primitive, abounding in spacious avenues that begin in nothing and lead nowhere."

In the presidential campaign of 1840, which began in March, Van Buren was a shoo-in for the Democratic nomination. Only two incumbent presidents had ever been defeated for reelection (John Adams in 1800, John Quincy Adams in 1828).

Close advisors warned the chief executive that the nation's economic troubles might cost him votes. Many banks had closed during the panic of 1837, and thousands of small businesses failed.

Treasury Secretary Levi Woodbury of New Hampshire begged the president to "avoid even the appearance of profligate spending." In a memo of November, 1839, he insisted that "We must convince the rank and file of voters that the tax dollar is spent with great care."

Depicted as riding Andrew Jackson's back, even then Van Buren was charged with having money on his mind while he went to the throne

That didn't stop Van Buren from requesting what he considered essential money. Alterations and repairs to the White House, plus purchase of furniture, trees, shrubs, and compost would cost $3,665.

Charles Ogle's attack upon the president's extravagance was printed in the *Congressional Register*. From that source it was reprinted and circulated as an official document.

Attacking what he called "The Royal Splendors of the President's Palace," the lawmaker posed a question: "Are honest citizens everywhere ready to maintain, for the private accommodation of the president, A ROYAL ESTABLISHMENT *at the cost of the nation*?

"Will they longer feel inclined to support their *chief servant* in a PALACE *as splendid as that of the Caesars, and as richly adorned as the proudest Asiatic mansion*?

"You may depend upon it something must be out of gear. The present occupant of the palace loves tassels, rosettes, and girlish finery almost as much as a real 'Bank Whig' loves 'hard cider.'"

Farmers, mechanics, and laborers were mocked for being so foolish as "to provide hay and pasturage for Mr. Van Buren's race and carriage horses." Nothing could be worse for the nation, continued the attack, than filling the president's house "with royal and imperial Wilton rugs, foreign cut wine coolers, French bedsteads, and one-hundred-dollar artificial flowers."

The cost of three White House curtains alone, said the congressman, "would build at least three goodly log cabins with money to spare."

Whigs seized upon the speech and elevated it into their chief campaign document. Sometimes in full but more often in fragments, it was reprinted hundreds of times—always with the notation that it was an official document of the U. S. Congress. In order to sharpen the contrast with big-spending Van Buren, William Henry Harrison was depicted as standing for "log cabins and hard cider."

Thrifty, hard-working Americans responded by turning Van Buren out of the White House. He lost even his home state and took just 60 electoral votes to Harrison's 234. "I was drunk down, sung down, and lied down," he said in summarizing the bitter campaign.

Regardless of how truth and falsehood were blended in Charles Ogle's speech, his exploitation of a request for $3,665 made that sum the biggest little amount ever to figure in a presidential election.

Early in the Reagan administration, political foes tried to capitalize upon the use of private gifts to refurbish and refurnish the White House. Even the charge that the president would be using "thousand-dollar dinner plates" made little impact. Just 140 years after Van Buren went down because he was portrayed as a big spender, typical Americans take "the imperial presidency" for granted.

Edison/Westinghouse "War of the Currents" Culminated in Sing Sing Prison

Late in the 1880s Thomas Edison and George Westinghouse were engaged in one of America's first—and most important—industrial wars. Electricity, not yet in general use, was widely considered "the energy with the greatest future." Edison had developed and was eager to market direct current equipment; Westinghouse favored alternating current and had invested everything he had in factories that would be worthless if that form of current failed to dominate the field.

In an atmosphere of high finance, industrial espionage, and rapid growth of the electrical industry its two giants brought their war to a climax on death row in Sing Sing prison.

Willie Kemmler, alias John Hart, lived in drab fashion and committed a wholly unimaginative crime by slaying his common-law wife with a hatchet. Though he never denied his guilt, when his trial began in May, 1889, newspapers of Buffalo, New York, intimated that it would be "sensational." Already there were rumors that if convicted, Kemmler might be the first man to face death by a new and untried process: electrocution. Eager for a way to make capital punishment humane, in 1888 New York lawmakers had passed an Electrical Death Act. Under its provisions any person executed after December 31 of that year would make "a fast and painless exit from the world through the power of electricity."

Language of the statute specified that *alternating current* should be used in the death house. Thomas Edison, already powerful and revered, was responsible for that clause. He and his colleagues had told lawmakers that alternating current—to which George Westinghouse had tied his future—was extremely lethal. His own system of low tension direct current, insisted the inventor, was virtually harmless—incapable of satisfactory use as a means of capital punishment.

New York State authorites, confronted with the necessity of putting together an instrument for quick and painless death by means of alternating current, knew of just one source from which to secure a dynamo. George Westinghouse himself rejected their overture. If his equipment should be used, publicity about its lethal effects could easily put him out of business.

Legislators had acted hastily and in ignorance, Westinghouse said. "The alternating current will kill, of course. So will dynamite and whisky, and lots of other things. But we have a system whereby such current can do no harm unless a man is fool enough to swallow a dynamo."

While Westinghouse balked and stalled, Edison and his cohorts went about the state staging public demonstrations designed to show the danger of alternating current. In these demonstrations, they put a number of animals to death. As yet, no word had entered standard use as a title for killing by electricity. *Scientific American* magazine noted that eighteen terms were competing for that place. Among them were: electromort; thanatelectrize, electrophony, electricide, voltacuss, fulmen—and electrocution.

Called by whatever name, the death of Willie Kemmler had to take place by means of an alternating current of electricity. That couldn't be done without the proper equipment. Since Westinghouse wouldn't supply it, perhaps his competitor would. A colleague of Edison, identified in documents of the era only as Harold P. Brown, allegedly got one of his clients in South America to order a Westinghouse dynamo. Once the machine was crated, it is said to have been re-sold two or three times in order to make it available to authorities at Sing Sing prison. There workmen began to build an electrically-wired chair whose design was already in the rough stage.

At this point the self-confessed killer received unexpected help. One of the greatest criminal lawyers of the era, W. Burke Cochran, came to the aid of Willie Kemmler. Since Kemmler clearly didn't have money enough to retain an attorney of note, it was widely believed that

Westinghouse paid the fees in order to try to halt the world's first electrocution.

All channels of appeal were exhausted. Kemmler's execution was set for August, 1890. Meanwhile, Brown had superintended completion of "the electric chair" and had tried it on animals. He told reporters that the death of the condemned man would come swiftly and painlessly because of the lethal power of the alternating current used.

He had a long list of men already accidentally killed "by running against the electric wires" he insisted. According to Brown, many of them had died from current produced by the Westinghouse dynamo—"the very machine that has been installed at Sing Sing." State Prison Superintendent Winthrop, who had followed the case closely, insisted that "death by electricity, using the alternating current, ushers in a new and humane era in the history of mankind."

Warden Durston of Sing Sing invited Dr. Carlos F. McDonald of the State Lunacy Commission to be present at the impending execution—which was to be followed by an immediate autopsy. Law officers, a justice of the state supreme court, two ministers and fourteen physicians were included among the twenty-seven witnesses permitted under New York law. All received secret messages to be on hand at daybreak on August 6.

No one—least of all Thomas Edison—dreamed that the execution of Willie Kemmler would receive more publicity and create more lasting impressions than any execution since King Louis XVI of France had died under the guillotine in 1793. For few executions have ever been so terribly botched.

Witnesses didn't have to be told when the shock of 1700 volts hit the condemned man. Pronounced dead after fifteen seconds, he soon began to sigh and struggle. There was at least one long burst of electricity after the head electrode had been strapped back in place; perhaps there were more. At any rate, current was not shut off until eight minutes after the switch was first thrown. Hair of the condemned man was singed. There was an odor of burnt flesh in the room. Numerous small blood vessels of his face had burst.

Public reaction was immediate and violent. As far away as London and Paris, newspapers condemned the "terrible torture." Experts and then members of the general public recognized that in spite of Edison's claims, alternating current couldn't possibly be lethal under all circumstances.

No one knows the total impact of that culmination of the "war of the currents" in Sing Sing. But every good biography of Edison and of Westinghouse includes references to otherwise forgotten Willie Kemmler. It took so long to kill him by means of alternating current that public support of Edison's system waned. People concluded that the Westinghouse current posed far less danger than they had been led to believe. Already, many engineers had stressed the AC-advantage of functioning with a transmission system far less costly than that for DC. Partly because of the swing in opinion that resulted from the highly-publicized first electrocution, morbid fear of alternating current vanished and it—rather than Edison's direct current—entered standard use in the U.S.

A Fugitive under Indictment for Murder Presided over the Senate Trial of Supreme Court Justice Samuel Chase

Supreme Court Justice Samuel Chase, impeached by the House of Representatives, was scheduled to be tried in February, 1805. Throughout the nation but especially in the capital, there was heated debate about the role played by Thomas Jefferson—who was eager for a conviction. As the date of the trial approached, the burning question of the day became: Who will preside?

Under ordinary circumstances that question would have been academic. But these were extraordinary times. In the election of 1800 Thomas Jefferson and Aaron Burr had received seventy-three votes each in the electoral college. Thrown into the House of Representatives in balloting that began on February 11, 1801, the contest was not decided for five days. On the thirty-sixth ballot, Jefferson was named president and Burr became vice-president. His chief Constitutional duty was that of presiding over the Senate.

There is some doubt that Aaron Burr was the perpetually-scheming totally-ambitious man depicted by some of his rivals. But he chafed in the role of vice-president, eagerly acted upon a chance to give up the post in order to occupy the New York governor's mansion—if elected chief executive of that state.

Badly beaten in the gubernatorial race, he was in no mood to tolerate attacks from his long-time rival Alexander Hamilton. Letters by three of Hamilton's friends, quoting him concerning Burr, had been made public in weeks before the election—and probably influenced its outcome. Hamilton, alleged Dr. Charles Cooper in a letter to General Philip Schuyler, had said that he regarded Burr "as a dangerous man, and one who ought not to be trusted with the reins of the government."

Sometime in June, 1804, published versions of that letter reached the vice-president. He wrote to Hamilton demanding an explanation but got what he considered an unsatisfactory reply. More exchanges of letters made things worse instead of better; Burr challenged Hamilton to meet him on the field of honor. Both men knew that a duel might lead to criminal charges—but neither would yield.

Five years earlier Burr had fought Hamilton's brother-in-law, John Barker Church, at Weehawk, New Jersey. Both men had missed with their first shot, and while the pistols were being reloaded Church had offered his opponent an apology that ended the fracas. Three years earlier Hamilton's eldest son, Philip, had been killed at Weehawk. What better place to end their enmity than on that bloody ground?

The place was settled, but not the time. It would be better, Hamilton proposed, to wait until the end of the term of the circuit court over which he was required to preside. Burr agreed. Once, on July 4, they sat next to one another at the banquet of the Society of the Cincinnati but were not observed to speak. July 11 was selected for the meeting, and both men made their wills. Samuel Bradhurst, a friend of Hamilton, tried to bring about a reconciliation—but succeeded only in prodding Burr into a duel with swords that left the Colonel with a prick in his arm.

Seconds settled upon a distance of ten paces, pistols not exceeding eleven inches in the barrel, and the determination of positions by lot. Both parties reached a ledge above the Hudson before 7 a.m. According to a document published next day by the seconds, "At the signal the fire of Colonel Burr took effect, and General Hamilton almost instantly fell." Burr was urged from the field to prevent recognition by the surgeon and bargemen who were approaching. At 2 p.m. on the following day, Hamilton died.

Burr fled to Philadelphia, lingered a few days and then accepted the invitation of Senator Pierce Butler to visit his plantation on St. Simon's Island, Georgia. Burr travelled under the name of R. King, in company with Samuel Swartwout and a slave named Peter. By now, he was a fugitive from justice.

Acting with unprecedented speed, a New York coroner's jury had on August 2 rendered a verdict of "Wilful murder." In weeks that followed, Governor Morgan Lewis and other men of influence pressed for a careful examination of the legal situation. As a result, New York dropped the murder charge for that of "challenging to a duel." Meanwhile New Jersey—on whose soil the fatal meeting had actually taken place—prepared to charge the vice-president with murder.

Burr remained in seclusion until late September, then proceeded toward Washington by leisurely stages. He reached the capital on November 4, already aware that a Bergen County, New Jersey jury had indicted him for murder. In his absence from home creditors had secured a court order under which his house and furniture had been sold to satisfy his debts.

A group of Congressional leaders drew up a round-robin petition asking Governor Bloomfield of New Jersey to quash the proceedings against Aaron Burr. Bloomfield (a friend of the fugitive) regretfully replied that under the constitution of the state, he had no power to take such action.

It was in this charged atmosphere that the nation's capital made preparation for the first trial of a Supreme Court Justice under impeachment. Few persons were neutral; they were either for Chase or against him. But with the vice-president a fugitive from the law, the city buzzed with gossip and speculation about who would preside over the trial.

Those questions were answered on February 4 when Aaron Burr took his seat in the Senate. Still under indictment for murder, he presided over the trial that brought a verdict of "Innocent" for Chase—a verdict that must have vexed Thomas Jefferson greatly. Still subject to possible extradition to New Jersey where he would have to answer for the death of Hamilton, Aaron Burr superintended the counting of electoral votes and personally handed parcels to tellers who reported a clear-cut second-term victory for Jefferson.

New Jersey authories never tried to extradite Burr, but he considered it "unwise" ever to enter the state. In New York he was disbarred and disenfranchised. Later tried for treason and acquitted, he returned to New York in 1812 and was permitted to resume the practice of law. During the last twenty-four years of his life, the man who had been among the most turbulent and controversial figures in American public life spent most of his time in his home, brooding over the past.

Samuel Langley's plane in flight, June 2, 1914

High Wind and Bad Luck Cost Samuel P. Langley the Renown Gained by the Wright Brothers

Just nine days before the Wright Brothers put their homemade *Flyer* into the air, a man with much more scientific knowledge and experience launched a machine that should have flown, but didn't. High wind and bad luck sent Samuel P. Langley's "aerodrome" spinning—and brought him ridicule instead of world fame.

Like Orville and Wilbur Wright, Langley was fascinated by science as a boy. "I cannot remember when I was not interested in astronomy," he said in later life. Born in Roxbury, Massachusetts, on August 22, 1834, he graduated from Boston High School—then launched a lifelong program of self-education. He learned so readily that after a period of work as an engineer and as an architect, in 1867 he was named director of Allegheny Observatory in Pittsburgh.

Several years before leaving Allegheny in 1887 in order to join the staff of the Smithsonian Institution, the self-taught scientist became keenly interested in the possibility of flight by heavier-than-air machines. He began by building models that were powered first by "India rubber," then by steam and by gasoline.

Successful performance by several models convinced him that he was on the right track. Meanwhile, he invented and built instruments that measured the lift and drift of moving plane surfaces. His findings led him to adopt curved supporting surfaces—successfully used in a four-wing power-driven model that looked much like an oversize dragonfly. Its wingspan was fourteen feet.

Experts who later studied his detailed notes concluded that by 1894 "Langley had mastered all the basic principles of aerodynamics and knew how to build a plane that would fly." One major obstacle remained. In this era, the lightweight gasoline engine didn't exist. All power plants then in use were too heavy for an airborne machine. So the engineer-scientist built his own light engines equipped with flash-boiler steam system heated by petrol and yielding about one horsepower for each five pounds of weight.

Early in 1896 Langley's Model #5, equipped with one of his engines and catapulted from a houseboat on the Potomac, flew about 3000 feet—until the fuel supply was exhausted. In November of the same year his Model #6 covered about 4200 feet. He was now ready to build a machine that would take a man into the air.

Unlike the Wright brothers, Langley had definite ideas about the future of the machine he called "aerodrome." He knew that observation balloons had been used during the Civil War, and insisted that a flying machine—whose pattern of flight could be controlled by its pilot—would revolutionize military tactics. He knew, too, that the French government was subsidizing Clement Ader's experiments aimed at producing just such a machine as he envisioned. It would take money—lots of money by standards of the era—to finance the machine that he envisioned.

Spurred by outbreak of the Spanish-American War, a joint Army-Navy Board agreed to let Assistant Secretary of the Navy Theodore Roosevelt outline Langley's plans and hopes. Response was overwhelmingly positive. Langley was voted $50,000 for "developing, constructing, and testing a flying machine capable of bearing a man." All the money was to be poured into the experiment; Langley was to give his own time and effort gratis.

Again the problem of finding a suitable power plant became paramount. Engines used successfully in models couldn't be adapted for larger and heavier machines. Veteran mechanic Charles M. Manley, who had joined Langley's team, went with him to Europe in order to look at auto engines in use and on the drawing boards of manufacturers. Nothing they saw was precisely what they wanted.

Back in Washington, Manley started from scratch and after extensive tests and adaptations put together an engine that yielded 53 horsepower at 950 rpm. Best of all, it weighed only a trifle more than 140 pounds.

Most of the money from military sources had been exhausted. To

Samuel P. Langley—the man who almost launched the airplane age

SAMUEL P. LANGLEY

complete his machine, Langley would have to get substantial backing from another source. It came from the Smithsonian Institution in a series of allocations that eventually came to a total of $23,000.

By 1903, Langley was sure he would get his machine into the air within the year. Complete with pilot, his aerodrome weighed slightly more than 800 pounds. With more than 1000 feet of sustaining surface and that lightweight 53 horsepower engine, the two pusher propellers would be more than adequate to give sustained and controlled flight.

July, 1903, saw the aerodrome dismantled and taken to a houseboat on the Potomac for reassembly. It was towed to a point forty miles below Washington, where the river is nearly three miles wide. But before launch day, a storm caused so much damage that the test had to be postponed for repairs. Wing ribs of the aerodrome were so badly warped that it took three months to get them back in shape. By then, winter was approaching and Langley was eager to test his machine.

Everything was ready on December 8, 1903. Again, however, the weather refused to cooperate. Very late in the afternoon tugs were brought into service to pull the houseboat so that it nosed directly into the wind. Newsmen, military observers, and a few members of Congress had assembled at Arsenal Point to see the flight.

At 4:45 p.m. pilot Charles Manley signalled for crewmen to release restraining pins so that the aerodrome would be thrown into the wind by means of a spring-driven catapult. Just as the pin was pulled, a sudden heavy gust sent the launching platform lurching. The rudder of the aerodrome—already in motion—was severely damaged. Though the machine cleared the rail, rear wings collapsed and it nosed into the water almost vertically.

That gust of wind ended Samuel P. Langley's attempts to put the aerodrome into the air. Wide publicity about his costly failure—heavily laced with ridicule—virtually obscured news that the Wright brothers successfully got their machine into the air just nine days after the disaster on the Potomac.

Until his death in 1906, Langley insisted that failure of his aerodrome stemmed from the launching process, not the machine's capacity to fly under its own power. Few persons outside a small circle of admirers took him seriously.

Eleven years after Langley failed to beat the Wright brothers into the air, Glenn H. Curtiss took the aerodrome to Lake Keuka, near Hammondsport, New York. Wary of a catapult launch because it

Langley's 1903 "aerodrome" was almost but not quite capable of flight; failure of the machine cost the inventor the support of Congressional appropriations

requires calm weather, he put "hydroaeroplane floats" under Langley's machine. Though they added more than 300 pounds, it was flown successfully on May 28, 1914, and several times later. Curtiss substituted one of his own 80-horsepower motors for Langley's and added another 400 pounds—then repeatedly flew the aerodrome "without damage to its delicate wing spars and ribs or excessive strain upon any part of the machine."

Prepared by fifteen years of scientific study of aerodynamics, backed by the U.S. military establishment and the Smithsonian Institution, and motivated by clear concepts of ways a heavier-than-air machine could become a new and decisive factor in war, Samuel P. Langley failed to become first to master the air only because of high wind and bad luck. When two rank amateurs succeeded nine days after his failure, their first acclaim came from the European rather than the American press.

Self-taught genius developed the only system of writing among American Indians

Use of the Printing Press by Cherokee Indians Was More than White Settlers Could Take

Spanish explorer-conqueror Hernando de Soto was the first European to have significant contact with native Americans who came to be called Cherokees. When he and his men marched through part of their country about 1540, they were town dwellers who generally lived in peace.

Even the Cherokees could not tell white men where or when they originated. They only knew that a Great Spirit, sometimes known as *Asga-Ya-Galun-Lati,* had been generous to them. He gave them land that spread from present-day Virginia through both Carolinas, Tennessee, Georgia and Alabama.

Initially, it was that 40,000 or so square miles of land that white men coveted. Vast tracts were seized by force. Under terms of a treaty drafted in 1802, the federal government was responsible for removing Cherokees from most or all of their holdings east of the Mississippi River.

While Washington waited to act, the Cherokees seized the initiative. They organized themselves into a nation, complete with a constitution, laws, and court system. Then they found attorneys who were willing to take their claims to the U. S. Supreme Court. Throughout the southeast, most whites rejoiced when the high court side-stepped the central issue by ruling that the Cherokees were not a real nation and hence could not sue.

Almost simultaneously, two separate sets of events sealed the fate of the Cherokees. One of those events, familiar to every reader of American history, was the discovery of substantial deposits of gold in Cherokee country. America's first gold rush, which began about 1829, had the effect of driving many native Americans from their pastures and hunting ranges. Now, more than ever, white men wanted all Indian land.

On February 21, 1828, the Cherokees gave the whites a good reason to fear them and to want them gone. That day at New Echota, temporary capital of the Cherokee Nation, American Indians produced the first issue of the first native-American newspaper. Called the *Cherokee Phoenix,* it was edited by a missionary but came into existence through the genius of a half-breed.

Before 1770 an Indian trader of German background, Nathaniel Gist, settled on North Carolina's Yadkin river. He made long forays into the heart of Cherokee country and sometimes stayed there for years at a time.

Somewhere in Tennessee, Gist fathered a male child by Wurteh, sister of a noted chief. Permanently crippled in childhood—perhaps by polio—George Gist (or Guess) came to be known to the white man as Sequoyah.

For a dozen years Sequoyah struggled to master the secrets of the "talking leaves" that gave white men such great advantages over Indians. He tried and discarded several systems of writing. Eventually he broke words down into syllables and reduced these to about 84 symbols. Now he had adequate tools with which to indicate every combination of sounds in every Cherokee word!

Cast into metal type, Sequoyah's symbols gave the Cherokees what no other native Americans had—the printed word. No wonder white-skinned settlers east and south of the Cherokee Nation viewed these developments with alarm!

It didn't take a lot of savvy to realize that a weekly newspaper printed in their own language would soon transform "a bunch of pesky trespassing varmints" into a cohesive nation. That nation would be doubly dangerous because it would be comprised of bucks and squaws who could actually read and write. Good land and gold-rich mountain streams aside, literate Cherokees were a special threat to hosts of white contemporaries who clumsily marked an "X" when asked to sign their names. To make matters worse, that first issue of the *Phoenix* included three articles from the newly adopted Cherokee Constitution.

Clearly, these people were digging in their heels to stay—permanently. They threatened the westward expansion of every state in which they held land.

At the famous battle of Horseshoe Bend in Alabama, Cherokee warriors had fought under the command of Andrew Jackson. One of them reputedly saved the life of the future president. Yet as chief executive of the United States, Jackson put all of his influence behind plans for removal of the Cherokees from their ancestral land. He was greatly influenced by officials of states whose citizens now feared the Cherokees more than ever. Having learned to read and write, they posed threats not even imagined earlier.

Money from the United States government was enough to persuade some Cherokee leaders to agree to go. They signed a treaty that required all tribesmen to move to new land west of the Mississippi River.

General Winfield Scott, commander in chief of the U. S. Army, brought troops to the Cherokee Nation. During a period of about two years, soldiers rounded up tribesmen and in 1838 drove the last 15,000 of them from their homes. About one-fourth of them died on the long journey that is famous as "The Trail of Tears."

Their printing press and their organization into a nation helped to make the Cherokees one of the most formidable of Indian threats to westward expansion of the white man's culture. Yet the Cherokees have had little success in their effort to gain legal redress for wrongs of the past, while other tribes and groups have won huge settlements from the U. S. Supreme Court. Ironically, these most advanced of native Americans didn't write into treaties precise descriptions and agreements upon which to base legal claims.

A Song by His Son-in-Law Saved John Tyler When the Nation's Biggest Naval Gun Exploded during an Excursion

On the afternoon of February 28, 1844, President John Tyler was headed toward the deck of the gunship *Princeton*. He stopped to listen to a military ditty sung by his son-in-law William N. Waller. As a result he was not among the notables who were killed or injured in the explosion of the 10-ton cannon dubbed the *Peacemaker*.

Though the U.S. was not yet a top naval power, in 1844 national leaders were eager to challenge European nations for mastery of the seas. That would be impossible so long as American vessels were limited in their firepower to pivot guns like those used on paddlewheel steamers.

Robert Field Stockton, a career naval officer, turned his attention to the problem of building bigger and better cannon. He found that cast iron ordnance (hard and brittle) was incapable of handling shot weighing more than 32 pounds.

Stockton shifted to wrought iron. With the new material he produced in England a smoothbore cannon, the *Oregon,* that fired 216-pound balls using charges of 20 and 30 pounds of powder. Qualified success of the *Oregon* led to the forging of a second 12-inch gun—this time produced in the U.S. by Ward and Co. Preliminary tests indicated that the *Peacemaker* was substantially stronger than the *Oregon*. When both powerful guns were mounted on the frigate *Princeton* the vessel became the pride of the U.S. Navy.

Captain Stockton pulled strings, twisted arms, and managed to arrange a "gala demonstration." National leaders, including the president, agreed to take an excursion down the Potomac River in order to see for themselves the power of the great guns.

As preparation for the day, a White House levee was held on the evening of February 27. Next morning, 150 ladies and 200 gentlemen crowded aboard the *Princeton*. Cabinet members jostled with foreign diplomats, senators and congressmen, plus the elite of Washington society. No one challenged Stockton's claim that the *Peacemaker* was the world's largest naval gun—and capable, by its might, of living up to its name.

A below-deck area, converted into an impromptu salon, was the center of activity for the morning. When most guests had eaten and drunk their fill, the *Princeton* weighed anchor and began to steam downstream about 1 p.m. Dignitaries crowded the decks in order to see and to hear the *Peacemaker* fired twice. Then at 3 p.m. most of them went back below decks for the "sumptuous collation" that had been prepared as part of the celebration. President Tyler himself proposed three separate toasts—one each to the United States Navy, the *Peacemaker,* and Captain Stockton.

Many more toasts followed, then some of the guests began to sing. Someone—never identified—mounted a table and shouted a proposal that the great cannon be fired once more in order to honor "The Father of our Country whose estate we shall soon be passing." Stockton nodded agreement and hurried above deck to order the necessary preparations. Many dignitaries trickled along behind them.

President Tyler was at the foot of the ladder when his son-in-law began to sing a military ditty. Tyler felt that it would be impolite to leave until the song was finished, so waited in company of Julia Gardiner who already expected to be asked to become his bride.

As Waller reached a line that ran "Eight hundred men lay slain," a roar announced that those who had tarried would not see the *Peacemaker* fired in honor of Washington. The words of the song were so singularly appropriate that listeners burst into applause. Then an officer "blackened with powder" dashed through the gangway and shouted: "Surgeons! All surgeons! To the deck! To the deck at once!"

At the blast intended to salute George Washington's memory, the breech of the *Peacemaker* had exploded. Jagged chunks of red-hot metal sprayed over the decks had wrought incredible havoc! Secretary of State Abel P. Upshur, who had given the go-ahead for construction and arming of the *Princeton* while serving as Secretary of the Navy, was dead. So was the present Secretary of the Navy, Thomas W. Gilmer. Senator David Gardiner, father of Tyler's future wife, lay in a pool of blood—killed instantly. Senator Thomas Hart Benton wandered about in a daze, his right eardrum ruptured. Commodore Beverly Kennon, chief of construction of the U.S. Navy, was dead. So was Virgil Maxcy, President Tyler's black body-slave. Two ablebodied seamen were killed on the spot; nine received serious injuries.

Badly shaken by what he called his "narrow and singular providential escape," President Tyler noted that the watch belonging to Senator Gardiner had stopped at 4:06—while the lawmaker's spectacles were not broken.

At 4:20 the *Princeton* reached Alexandria, where the steamer *I. Johnson* took most survivors aboard. With Secretary of War William Wilkins, Tyler remained aboard the stricken vessel until 8:10 p.m. Bodies of victims were left there for the night, then taken to the East Room of the building that was still commonly designated simply as "the President's house."

James G. Birney, candidate for the presidency as leader of the Liberty Party, noted that "our fair capital has seen nothing quite like the funeral services conducted with quiet solemnity on Saturday, March 2.

"Many mourners who are political rivals of John Tyler join his admirers in wonder," said Birney, "at the marvel of the way in which a military song delivered him from imminent danger of sudden death or crippling injury."

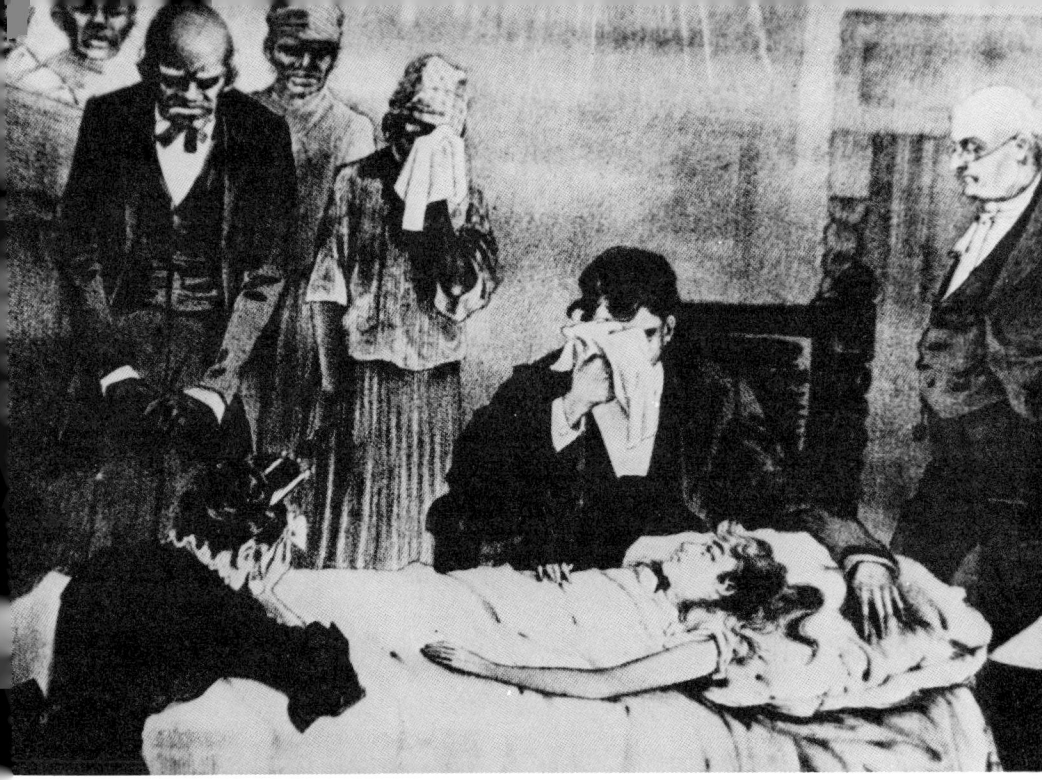

UNCLE TOM'S CABIN—*detail from poster advertising production of "Stover's Great Mammoth Uncle Tom Cabin Co." —circa 1885*

America's Most Successful and Influential Drama Was Taken to the Stage against the Wishes of the Author

Forty-year-old Harriet Beecher Stowe didn't have the foggiest idea of how it would affect the nation when in 1851 she began publishing a serial in the anti-slavery *National Era* of Washington, D.C. Her announced purpose was to give a faithful portrayal of everyday life among slaves in the south—about whom she had little firsthand knowledge. *Uncle Tom's Cabin; or, Life Among the Lowly,* was the end result. Practically forgotten today, the subtitle expressed the real intentions of the author.

Struggles over copyright law, brought into sharp focus during the

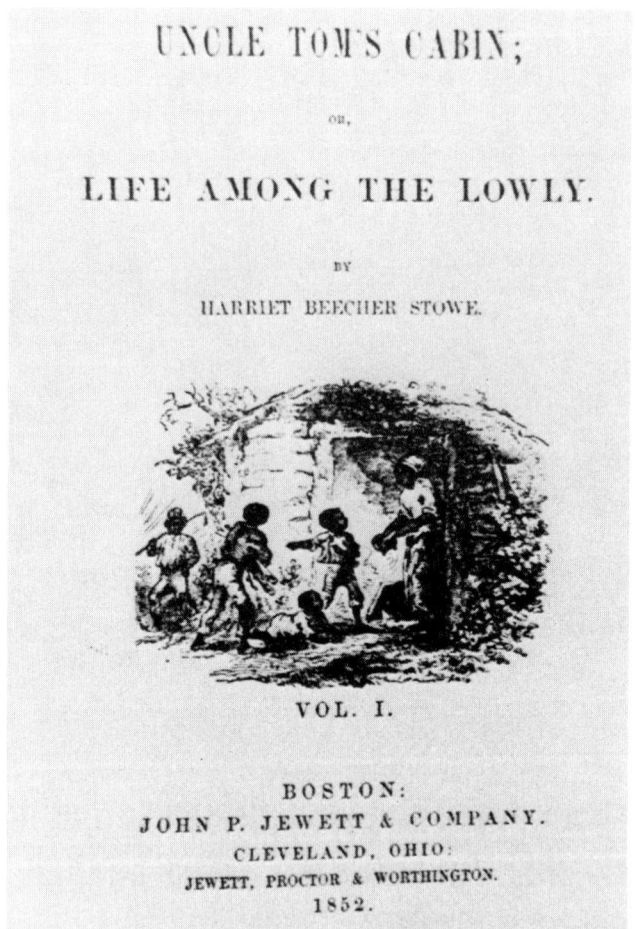

Title page of first English edition of history-making novel whose subtitle is now seldom remembered

1970s by the proliferation of photocopy equipment, hadn't yet been fought in the 1850s. Copyright of a published literary work gave the author no rights in dramatized versions, and no control over them. So it was purely perfunctory—a courtesy on his part—when popular singer Asa Hutchinson requested Mrs. Stowe's permission to prepare a dramatic version of her novel that still had many weeks to run as a newspaper serial.

Harriet Beecher Stowe flatly rejected the proposal. Many—perhaps most—of her biographers conclude that she did so on religious grounds. Daughter of Presbyterian clergyman Lyman Beecher and sister of Congregational clergyman Henry Ward Beecher, there's no doubt that she appealed to piety in her refusal.

". . . any attempt on the part of Christians to identify themselves with (theatrical productions) will be productive of danger to the individual character, and to the general cause," she told Hutchinson.

Did that language faithfully express the reason for her views . . . or was it a piously-worded excuse? From the perspective of more than a century, much evidence supports the latter view.

Her letters include many allusions to the theater. She was eager to know what her daughters thought about Sarah Bernhardt. She referred dispassionately to *The Black Crook*—a musical that was anathema to many church folk because of the "nakedness" it exploited. During a period spent in Florida with her daughters she joined them in sponsoring both "dancing parties" and dramatic performances. She spoke with approval about views of actresses such as Sarah Siddons and Adelaide Ristori. Gossip among the devout of Andover, Massachusetts, had it that she actually attended plays in Boston.

Vigorous, colorful, and dramatic she clearly was. Prudish by standards of the era, she clearly was not. So her refusal to sanction a theatrical version of her novel could have stemmed from fear—never publicly expressed—that dramatists and actors would somehow distort her message and destroy her characters. If that actually was the unspoken basis for her opposition to putting her story and her people on the boards, she was incredibly farsighted. Distortion began almost at once, during the 1850s, and reached a climax during the 1890s when as many as 400 to 500 troupes were devoting themselves entirely to the money-making art of "Uncle Tomming."

Harriet Beecher Stowe's original Uncle Tom was strong in his gentleness—eager not to placate his white master, but to gain entrance into the Kingdom of Heaven. Transformed under the impact of thousands of dramatic appearances by second- or third-rate actors, he became the boot-licking old man whose name entered general speech to indicate a toady willing to endure anything with the hope of saving his own skin. Bloodhounds on the ice, as handled by Jay Rial's Ideal drama group and scores of others, came to mean more to the audience than the underlying message of the novel that gave Little Eva to the world. A single glance at a playbill designed to lure listeners to the theater in order to hear Mrs. C. C. Howard sing "Oh! I'se So Wicked" gives proof positive that the Topsy of the theater was a quite different person from the Topsy of the novel.

Among dramatists, only Asa Hutchinson seems even to have asked for permission to stake a claim to the literary gold mine that was offered to the public in the form of a novel. Before final installments of *Uncle Tom* had appeared in the *National Era,* a play based on the story was being performed in Baltimore.

No dramatic version was ever sanctioned by Harriet Beecher Stowe, and she never collected a dime in royalties. But the play, complete with bloodhounds, hit the ground running and continued to gain momentum for half a century. Public clamor for it was, if possible, even greater than that for the phenomenally successful novel.

First issued in book form by J. P. Jewett of Boston in a then-ambitious edition of 10,000 copies, *Uncle Tom* sold out within a week of its appearance on March 20, 1852. By May, it had been issued in London. There was no international copyright convention to protect rights of the author, so English, German, Scottish, French, and Italian publishers pirated as they pleased. No one knows how many copies were sold. Jewett alone issued 300,000 during the first year and competitors brought out at least three times as many. By 1893 the British

Manuscript page of "Uncle Tom" (fascimile)

Museum held copies in Armenian, Bohemian, Danish, Dutch, Finnish, Flemish, French, German, Hungarian, Italian, Polish, Portugese, Greek, Russian, Spanish, Swedish, and Welsh—plus dozens of English-language editions and "versified or dramatized adaptations, extracts, and abridgements."

Proliferation of dramatized versions of *Uncle Tom* proceeded even more rapidly than that of printed ones. By 1854 New York alone saw simultaneous offerings at Purdy's National Theater, Barnum's American Museum, Christy's Minstrels, the Bowery Theater and the Franklin Museum. Each promoter tended to publicize his as "the only authentic version."

Actually, though, few promoters and few if any long-time performers made any effort to preserve the spirit and mood of Harriet Beecher Stowe's novel. Instead there was constantly jostling for "audience effect"—achieved by modification of dialogue, simplification of story line, and by putting players into stereotyped roles.

The public didn't care that pursuit of Eliza by bloodhounds was a dramatic device foreign to the novel. And in the atmosphere of national tension produced by the slavery issue, there was genuine clamor for villains who were very villainous and for heroes who were bigger-than-life by virtue of the obstacles they faced.

If bloodhounds were suddenly at a premium, so were Uncle Toms. Demand for men adept in the title role was so great that a Chicago theatrical agency dropped all other interests and specialized in finding Uncle Toms. Some of them spent most of their adult lives playing that one role. Many enlisted members of their families, who joined the cast and travelled for weeks or for years offering the public nothing except *Uncle Tom*. Simultaneously, dozens of professional "Uncle Tommers" played in London, Edinburgh, Berlin, Paris, and other cities where the Ohio River meant nothing more than a wandering line on a map of a far-off place.

Appetite for the dramatized version of "the novel that started the Civil War" diminished after the turn of the 20th century, but never vanished altogether. Mason Brothers' company, in its 57th season, was still "Uncle Tomming" in 1927. Edwin S. Porter pioneered with a movie version made for the Edison Co. in 1903; since then at least a dozen more have been put on film. Carl Laemmle's $2,500,000 version almost—but not quite—broke box-office records made by 1923 versions of *The Hunchback of Notre Dame* and *The Ten Commandments*.

As this broadside indicates, the worst fears of Harriet Beecher Stowe were realized; on stage, her epic characters were often made to appear comical.

Whether rendered by a "family troupe" stopping in Kokomo, Indiana, for a one-night stand in 1854 or by veteran actors performing before cameras, no dramatic version has been truly faithful to the novel from which it was drawn. No matter what her motives may have been, Harriet Beecher Stowe was right in withholding her name from *Uncle Tom's Cabin* in the flesh. Yet measured by any standard it is far and away the most successful and influential of American dramas. Critic-historian Edward Wagenknecht may be right in judging that, warts and all, the stage version of *Uncle Tom* "was the closest approach to folk drama that America ever made."

Charles James Fox, as satirized by the noted cartoonist, Gillray

During the American Revolution, America Had Hosts of Friends and Supporters in Great Britain

From the beginning of tension until the final treaty of peace between Britain and the new United States of America, colonists had more friends than foes in the homeland. London—then far the largest metropolitan center in the western world—was solidly against all anti-American measures. So were merchants, businessmen, and ordinary citizens throughout Britain.

Some of England's most brilliant orators repeatedly spoke out against the king and his ministers. But members of the House of Lords held their seats by virtue of their aristocratic heritage, not by election.

Many (but not all) of them supported those anti-American leaders who said that it was right to launch and then to continue the war.

Irish-born Edmund Burke (1729–1797) emerged as an eloquent friend of America long before the Declaration of Independence was issued. His views of "the American question" propelled him into prominence in the Whig party. It nearly always opposed what King George III wanted to do.

Burke spoke in Parliament in the spring of 1774, urging repeal of the tax on tea. A few months later he opposed the bills that called for closing the port of Boston and annulling the Massachusetts charter.

For the pro-American lawmaker, though, his shining hour came on March 22, 1775. That day he spoke for 3 hours urging a policy of conciliation toward the Colonies. "It is not what a lawyer tells me I may do," he insisted, "but what humanity, reason, and justice tell me I ought to do."

Since he was opposing the king and his cabinet, Burke probably knew that Parliament wouldn't adopt his measures *On Conciliation*. But two centuries later the British magazine, *History Today*, said that the famous speech "is known to every schoolboy" in the island kingdom.

Charles James Fox (1749–1806) is less widely known to Americans than Burke. Though less eloquent than his colleague, he was equally stubborn. He publicly and loudly opposed the official governmental position from the time of the Boston Tea Party. Britain's tax on tea destined for the New World was, said he, "a mere assertion of a right which would force the colonists into open rebellion."

In October, 1774, Fox censured the king's ministers for adding to the discontent in America. "The king of Prussia, nay, Alexander the Great, never gained more in one campaign than the noble lord [North — British prime minister during the 1770's] has lost; he has lost a whole continent," said Fox.

Following the Colonial victory in the battle of Saratoga, Fox was so bluntly pro-American that fellow lawmaker Henry H. Luttrell said he was talking treason. *The Morning Post*—a most influential newspaper controlled by King George—taunted Fox because he had not challenged Luttrell to a duel. Tone of the newspaper piece was such that some Members of Parliament "suspected that there was a scheme to get rid of Fox by provoking a duel."

America's friend in Britain refused to be goaded into exchanging shots with his political foe. But he adopted the habit of referring to the king as "Satan." Once he publicly remarked that "Certainly things look well, but he [King George III] will die soon, and that will be best of all." Probably correctly, Fox over and over insisted that the Parliamentary majority in favor of war with the Colonies existed only because many lawmakers were eager to please the king.

Governmental leaders who held their posts through royal appointment or influence were joined by cartoonists and writers of pamphlets who jeered at America's friends.

Among such friends, none was more colorful than John Wilkes (1727–1797). As an outspoken foe of the king and his policies and a champion of colonial rights, Wilkes was 3 times expelled from membership in the House of Commons. But he sued the secretary of state for illegal arrest—and won. He became Lord Mayor and then Chamberlain of London, and finally got his name cleared in 1779 so that he could again debate and vote in Parliament.

Through Wilkes' influence, prominent Londoners formed the Society of Supporters of the Bill of Rights. Wilkes helped to manipulate events that triggered public demonstrations and riots. In return he was arrested on a "general warrant" (a warrant in which the name of no individual is mentioned) and was thrown in jail.

While the English political leader was behind bars, the House of Assembly of South Carolina sent him £1,500. In Boston the Sons of Liberty drank toasts to him when they gathered at Liberty Tree in order to hail him as "the illustrious martyr of liberty."

Wilkes and other pro-American spokesmen made political hay from King George's employment of German mercenaries, plus the extensive use of "Red Indian savages," in the war with American colonists. "Even loyalist sentiment was shocked" by such actions, according to an early edition of the *Encyclopedia Britannica.*

In contrast to Wilkes, who was "a man of the people," wealthy Thomas William Coke of Norfolk (1752–1842) laid his fortune on the line for America. He actually hated and despised King George III, largely because the ruler insisted on prosecuting the American War against the opposition of a majority of British citizens of all classes.

King George once expressed a desire to visit Coke's palatial country estate, Holkham Hall. The pro-American owner tartly sent word to the monarch that the house was open to the public every Tuesday.

An old rule that hadn't been observed for generations stipulated that only the king could drive around London in a coach drawn by 6 horses. When George III began trying to enforce that edict, Coke repeatedly drove past the royal palace in a coach pulled by 5 horses and a donkey.

Jonathan Shipley, who was as outspoken as Wilkes, never quite recovered from setbacks given him because he, too, echoed the cry of Britain's common folk to stop badgering the Colonists in America.

Shipley (1714–1788) studied for the priesthood and seemed destined to become the head of the Church of England. But just as he was gaining national renown the king's policies toward the American colonies caused the churchman to join those opposed to the king. His shift in position is believed to have been brought about as an effect of an

John Wilkes

early and long-lasting friendship with Benjamin Franklin. Franklin was Shipley's house guest as early as 1771, and while visiting there wrote part of his famous *Autobiography.*

"I look upon North America as the only great nursery of free men left on the face of the earth," Shipley told fellow members of the House of Lords in 1774. When a new Archbishop of Canterbury had to be chosen, even the great Horace Walpole regarded him as "the likeliest man." But King George moved swiftly and suddenly to give the post to one of his own supporters. Long-standing tradition holds that Shipley "would have been archbishop, had he abandoned his opposition to the war."

William Pitt, Earl of Chatham (1708-1778), still ranks as one of England's all-time great orators. He won that reputation while speaking in Parliament in defense of the Americans. During a period of severe illness, in May, 1777, Pitt tried to persuade Parliament to demand that the war be ended.

"You may ravage," he warned, "but you cannot conquer. It is impossible. You cannot conquer the Americans. I might as well talk of driving them before me with this crutch."

Usually the king and his ministers could muster enough votes to defeat any pro-American measure. Occasionally, as in November, 1775, so many elected members of Parliament deliberately stayed away that there was no quorum for a vote. Many of them agreed with Burke that proposals made by Lord Frederick North, head of the British cabinet, constituted "a method of ransom by auction." Most of those who refused to take their seats so that a vote could be taken on one of North's measures had nodded assent when Burke had thundered: "The Americans will have no interest contrary to the grandeur and glory of England when they are not oppressed by the weight of it. Loyal subjects of His Majesty need not apprehend the destruction of this empire by giving, as an act of free grace and indulgence, to 2,000,000 of my fellow citizens [in the colonies] some share of those rights we have been taught to value for ourselves."

Burke, Pitt, Shipley, Wilkes, Fox, and other persons of influence seem never to have made the slightest progress in trying to influence the views of King George III. But according to *British History Illustrated* magazine, they did affect the views of substantially more than half of the ordinary folk of Britain.

Throughout the island kingdom as well as in faraway America,

An anonymous artist depicted Wilkes as exemplifying fortitude, about to be crowned after being stabbed

the attempt to enforce obedience by military might was dubbed "the king's war." Had only a handful of men in key places of power been willing to listen to a star-studded group of leaders who begged for compromise instead of bloodshed, there would have been no American Revolution of the sort which actually erupted at the time.

The first modern sleeping car, added to Lincoln's funeral train at the behest of his widow, was dubbed "The Pioneer"

Lincoln's Funeral Train Boosted the Pullman Car into Acceptance that Led to Dominance of the Rails

Mary Todd Lincoln passed through Chicago in an 1865 railroad journey to Springfield. Tradition has it that while waiting between trains the wife of the president was invited to take a look at the world's most elegant and expensive railroad car. She left no account of her on-the-spot impressions of the magnificent *Pioneer*—complete with Brussels carpet, many ornate mirrors, hand-carved cherry woodwork, and radically new system of berths for sleeping. Clearly, however, Mrs. Lincoln was greatly impressed by the *Pioneer* because a few months later when the train bearing the body of her martyred husband pulled out of

Chicago on the last leg of its long and mournful journey, she insisted that the *Pioneer* be attached for her personal use.

Both in Europe and in the U.S. rapid expansion of railroads had led farsighted men to experiment with cars that would permit passengers to sleep while they rode. Colonel William D'Alton Mann organized the Compagnie Internationale des Wagons-Lits to supply "boudoir cars" with compartments for four or for two passengers. T. T. Woodruff of the Terre Haute & Alton built and put into service a series of sleepers that had six sections on each side.

Former wagonmaker Webster Wagner, working for Vanderbilt's sprawling New York Central line, built cars with berths plus linen compartments for exclusive use on rails controlled by the Commodore. These and other early sleeping cars were crowded, rough, and uncomfortable. Passengers slept fully clothed and fought to hold their berths when cars lurched around sharp curves or jolted along rough sections of track.

In 1858 an ambitious young entrepreneur who had left school at age fourteen spent what he called "a comfortless night" on a sleeping car during a sixty-mile journey from Buffalo to Westfield, New York, returning for a visit to Chautauqua County where he had been born and reared. That night, George Mortimer Pullman decided that he could—

Pullman—father of the modern railway sleeping car

and would—design and build a sleeping car whose primary concern would be comfort of passengers.

Pullman was totally without car-building experience, but had a vivid imagination and plenty of nerve. Many who came in contact with him during his youth called him "brash." That title was first applied to him when, not old enough to grow a full beard, he had offered to take on a job that veteran engineers thought impossible. Widening of the Erie Canal—popularly derided as "DeWitt Clinton's Ditch"—became necessary very early in the 1850s. Owners of buildings along the margins of the ditch wanted them moved instead of torn down. Experts said it couldn't be done; young Pullman offered to try. He succeeded so well at house-moving that he built up about $6,000 in capital—enough to look for greener fields.

Chicago was ready to begin raising itself out of the swamp in which it had been built. Streets posed no major problems. But large buildings such as the Tremont hotel appeared to be doomed. Young Pullman appeared on the scene, offered to raise the four-story Tremont "without breaking a pane of glass" and got the contract. Using 5,000 jackscrews and 12,000 workmen, he made the job seem easy.

Since the Windy City was already becoming a major rail center, the New Yorker who made his money raising buildings decided to sink some of it in sleeping cars that would be more comfortable than the one he remembered so vividly. Officials of the Chicago & Alton Railroad, who had only a dozen day coaches, let Pullman convert two of them to sleepers. In them he installed hinged upper berths whose position could be altered by means of pulleys and ropes. Each car had two wood-burning stoves and passengers were provided with pillows and blankets.

Though these early cars were mildly successful, Pullman was far from satisfied with them. Six-foot ceilings made them seem cramped, and berths too short for a tall man added to this impression. It cost about $1,000 to convert each day coach and new "rattlers" built for Vanderbilt's line involved an investment of about $4,000 each. George Pullman envisioned a much bigger, much better—and far more expensive—sleeper.

By 1864 he was ready to take the plunge. With boyhood friend Ben Field as a partner, he sank a colossal $18,000 into *The Pioneer*. By far the most costly railroad car then in existence, it stood two and one-half feet higher than conventional cars and was a full foot wider. The

Interior of conventional railroad coach, built in 1865, in which passengers who traveled all night had to sleep sitting upright (Baltimore & Ohio R.R. coach)

Pioneer was equipped with hinged upper berths plus hinges that made it possible to slide the seat forward and the back down. Covered by patents # 42,182 and #49,992, these innovations produced the world's first real sleeping car—whose seats and berths could be folded for daytime travel.

So much money had been invested in the luxurious sleeper that it would never pay for itself unless passengers were charged $2.00 per night instead of the standard $1.50. Most railroad executives were wary of such high fares. And elegant as it was, *The Pioneer* couldn't be put into service. It was too wide and too tall.

In the language of railroad historian Stewart Holbrook, "the death of President Lincoln dropped into Pullman's lap a wondrous opportunity." For when the president's widow asked to use *The Pioneer* on the last leg of the journey that took the special funeral train from Washington to Springfield, officials of the Chicago & Alton got busy. Working around the clock, special crews cut platforms and widened bridges so that Pullman's wide car could squeeze by. At many points, overhead girders were raised in order to accommodate the car that towered two feet above ordinary ones.

Scheduled to leave Chicago at 9:30 p.m. on May 2, 1865, Lincoln's funeral train—with *The Pioneer* at the rear—pulled out while bells of the city were tolling. All through the night, bonfires glowed at intervals along the track. All telegraph stations were kept open continuously while crossings were guarded by crews equipped with lanterns and flags. A pilot engine ran ahead of the funeral train, keeping no less than eight and no more than twelve minutes ahead.

On that sorrowful journey *The Pioneer* made a great impression on notables aboard the funeral train. One of them, General U.S. Grant, a few months later requested and got permission to use *The Pioneer* on a journey to his home in Galena, Illinois. Again, platforms and bridges were altered—and another line was open to the luxurious sleeper destined to make "Pullman" a household word.

Propelled into the national spotlight at the whimsy of a president's widow whose every wish was honored during the time of national mourning, Pullman's huge car came to be such a symbol of luxurious travel that line after line adapted equipment to accommodate it. Slowly at first, then more and more rapidly, additional Pullman cars were built. By the end of the century they had become a standard feature of U.S. railway travel.

Washington was recognized by election to the Hall of Fame

Supreme Diplomat Booker T. Washington Was Castigated as "A Half-Load Leader"

On July 4, 1881, thirty-odd black males gathered under a chinaberry tree on Zion Hill, Tuskegee, Alabama. Under ordinary circumstances, white villagers might have called a parley of their own. This time they did not. Everyone in the community knew that this was the first day of the new black school.

Though the lone teacher was from 'way up north in West Virginia, two local men had paved the way for his coming.

Banker-merchant George Campbell was white; shoemaker, tinsmith, and harness maker Lewis Adams was black. It was Adams

Tuskegee students literally raise the roof for a new college building

who'd conceived the idea of starting a trade school for members of his race. So the ex-slave told former slave owner Campbell of his dream — and asked for help.

Campbell had influential friends. With their help Alabama legislators were persuaded to set aside $2,000 for one year's operation of a school. Chartered on Lincoln's birthday (February 12, 1881) it had no formal name. Nor was there a gnat's chance that any Alabama black could get the school going.

That's why a joint letter from Adams and Campbell went to far away Hampton Institute in Virginia. There General Samuel C. Armstrong had won a national reputation as a teacher of blacks. Could he — would he — recommend someone to head the Alabama experiment?

General Armstrong suggested only one name: Booker T. Washington, a Hampton student for three years, ending in 1875.

Born near Hale's Ford, Virginia, in April, 1856, young Booker had no father and no surname. According to talk in the slave cabins he was the son of a white man from a neighboring plantation. He gave himself his surname.

Having moved with his mother and stepfather to Malden, West

Virginia, in 1865, he got his first taste of schooling. His teacher, a black veteran of the Union Army, held night classes for boys who worked at salt furnaces and in coal mines by day.

"'Booker' won't do, boy," insisted the teacher when his new pupil came to enroll. "You gotta have a real name. Tell me—'Booker' who?"

Swallowing hard, the 9-year-old decided he might as well aim as high as he could. "'Washington,' sir," he said: "Booker T. Washington!"

He took that name with him in 1872 when he traveled, mostly on foot, 500 miles to Hampton Institute. There he was handed a broom and told to sweep a room as his admission test.

Recalling that all-important day in later life, he often said: "I swept that room just three times—but when I put down the broom, I dusted it four times!"

At the school whose motto was "Learn by Doing," he mastered the brick mason's trade. He learned to use a toothbrush, and for the first time in his life slept between sheets. He completed his studies and returned home to teach. Three years later he took the great challenge and went to Alabama.

Tuskegee Normal and Industrial Institute, as he named the school, had a budget of $2,000 for its first year's operation. There was no building, not an acre of land.

Black members of a local church lent the use of a shanty. Then Washington borrowed $500 from Hampton Institute as half payment for 100 acres of land and a few tumbledown outbuildings.

Blacks and whites alike contributed. Some gave money. A prosperous black farmer gave a hog, and a white neighbor contributed an old, blind horse.

Three brick kilns failed. Washington pawned his watch for $15 in order to build a fourth—and saw fine, hard bricks pour from it by the thousand. Students built Porter Hall with their own hands, thereby starting a tradition that Tuskegee would expand by letting young men learn by doing.

Washington placed so much emphasis upon manual skills that some members of his race derided him as an Uncle Tom—"a half-loaf leader" who promised education and provided work.

At the Cotton States Exposition of 1895 in Atlanta, Tuskegee's founder was the first black speaker to electrify a predominantly white Southern audience. They cheered because he frankly accepted the *status quo*.

In his famous book, *An American Dilemma,* noted sociologist Gunnar Myrdal calls Washington "the supreme diplomat of the Negro people through a generation filled with severe trials, who was able by studied unobtrusiveness to wring so many favors from the white majority."

Visiting railroad magnate Collis P. Huntington, Washington was brushed aside while being handed two dollars. The Alabama educator thanked Huntington — then came back, and back again. Once he got $50,000. Another visit yielded enough money to build Huntington Hall.

It was the gentle black man with the big, strong hands who interested Andrew Carnegie and Julius Rosenwald in blacks of the south. Harvard University presented Washington with the first honorary degree awarded to a black. Washington's likeness went into the American Hall of Fame, at New York University, in 1946.

His methods wouldn't work today. But his critics tend to overlook the possibility that *only* his methods would have worked in the rural south in 1881.

Long since coeducational, Tuskegee Institute is no longer primarily "industrial." Most black veterinarians in the United States studied

Tuskegee's annual Farmers' Institute was the first of its sort in the South

Booker T. Washington addressing the National Cotton Exposition in Atlanta in 1895. In this speech he was cheered by an all-white audience for his acceptance of the "half-loaf leader" role

there. So did engineers, nurses, architects, chemists, and hosts of distinguished persons with other special training.

Having celebrated her centennial in 1981, Tuskegee today remains "the lengthened shadow of one man"—her founder, whom scholars credit with having influenced white public opinion even more than black.

Illustrations in this chapter were provided by the courtesy of Tuskegee Institute.

The Great Dynamite Conspiracy

The Accused Labor Leaders, the Man Who Accuses Them and the Scene of the Outrages That Shocked a Continent

Photos above a June, 1911, news story showed Burns, left, with boyish-looking labor leader McNamara who claimed he was merely a target for anti-labor capitalists

Dynamite Explosions in Now-Forgotten Labor Wars Propelled Private Detective William J. Burns into World Fame

From early 1905 to late 1910, sixteen U.S. states were gripped in a now-forgotten labor war over the issue of the closed shop. At least eighty-six explosions took place during the period. Railroad bridges were destroyed or damaged. Big stockpiles of structural material were made useless. With dynamite and nitroglycerin, the standard explosives of the era, losses ran into many millions of dollars. Labor-management tensions mounted because many union leaders insisted that owners were deliberately destroying their own plants in order to make labor look bad, while owners pressed for the arrest and conviction of labor leaders whom they blamed for the wave of destruction.

On October 1, 1910, the three-story building of the Los Angeles *Times*—published by bitterly anti-labor Harrison Gray Otis—exploded and then crumbled. Few of the nearly one hundred men working the early-morning shift escaped without injury; twenty of them died on the spot or in hospitals to which they were taken. Otis borrowed presses to issue a one-sheet extra devoted exclusively to the wholly unsupported charge that "UNIONIST BOMB WRECKS THE 'TIMES' ".

In the fever heat of public reaction, Los Angeles Mayor George B. Alexander departed from accepted procedures. At taxpayers' expense he retained private detective William J. Burns to enter the case in cooperation with the San Francisco Police Department.

Born in Baltimore in 1861 and reared in Ohio, Burns had become a detective purely by chance. When his father became police commissioner of Columbus, Ohio, William saw an opportunity to pick up some extra money by helping authorities solve mysterious crimes. That led him into investigation of election frauds and then into the U.S. Secret Service. In 1909 he left the federal payroll in order to join William P. Sheridan in forming the Burns & Sheridan Detective Agency, with headquarters in Chicago. Sheridan sold out the following year, so the always-flambouyant Burns changed the name of his organization to the William J. Burns National Detective Agency.

In that era there were no TV shows to extoll the prowess and virtues of the private eye. Many who accepted cases without the authority of a badge to support them ran afoul of the law. Ordinary citizens tended to rank private detectives with, or at most just one cut above professional criminals. Burns was called into the San Francisco case largely because he had broken an important case there while still a member of the Secret Service.

When he accepted the case he had no idea that it would become a *cause celebre* in the organized labor movement. Nor did he dream that it would generate a steady flow of page-one news for fifteen months, frequent headlines for another three years, and cause the nation's most prominent criminal lawyer to promise never again to plead a case in California.

From the start, it was clear that the destruction of the *Times* building was deliberate rather than accidental. But the devastation was so great that techniques of the era were not sufficiently refined to enable investigators to find fragments of the bomb. The case might have been closed as an unsolved mystery had not strage suitcases been delivered on the morning of the explosion to the homes of publisher Otis and the secretary of the Merchants and Manufacturers Association—roughly equivalent to today's Chamber of Commerce. One suitcase exploded when detectives tried to open it, but the other yielded dynamite of the type used in quarry work plus a cheap alarm clock and a network of wires.

Burns had investigated an apparently unrelated bombing in Peoria, Illinois, just three weeks before the *Times* blew up. In the Illinois case there was property damage to the steel firm of McClintock, Marshall & Co., but no loss of life. Burns and his men were puzzled, though, at the coincidence by which the same type of high-grade dynamite had been used in both instances. Clearly, too, a skilled professional had been involved in Illinois as well as in California. Unreliable fulminating caps were then in general use. But both at the steel works and the newspaper plant it appeared that dynamiters had used a direct electrical spark activated by some sort of timekeeping device.

A break in the Peoria case led Burns to Ortie McManigal of Indianapolis, Indiana. He, in turn, led the detective to "J. B. Bryce"—who turned out to be James B. McNamara. In itself, identification of McNamara was not significant. But the suspect was the younger brother of the Indianapolis-based International Association of Bridge and Structural Iron Workers. Iron workers were noted for their activity in strike-breaking—and a disproportionate number of unsolved dynamitings had involved steel mills, steel bridges, and buildings in which steel girders were employed.

By late April Burns had a mass of circumstantial evidence plus McManigal's promise to give state's evidence with the hope of getting a light sentence. (Plea bargaining, in the contemporary sense, hadn't yet become an accepted practice.) McManigal's testimony, alone, seemed adequate to secure convictions. Burns moved so swiftly that he himself probably disregarded the law more than once, but late in April he arrested John McNamara in Detroit.

Arrest of the union leader made headlines in Europe as well as throughout the U.S.—and triggered a wave of support for the accused man. Longtime A. F. of L. president Samuel Gompers launched and quickly completed a drive to raise a defense fund of $300,000. Clarence

Strongly pro-McNamara crowds waiting to glimpse labor leaders on December 1, 1911, did not know that on that day they had entered pleas of guilty.

Darrow was retained to defend the brothers McNamara. A hastily-produced and emotion-charged movie, which pictured the labor leaders and associates as victims of a conspiracy, was exhibited wherever organized labor was strong. Darrow argued that the arrest and extradition of John McNamara were extra-legal, and persuaded an Indianapolis grand jury to indict Burns on a kidnapping charge.

In this climate practically everyone including Burns expected an early acquittal when jury selection began in October, 1911. There was no doubt about public sentiment in Los Angeles. Pro-McNamara banners, buttons, and newspaper editorials generated a great deal of enthusiasm. Anarchists—known to have a liking for San Francisco—were generally felt to have been responsible for the dynamiting of the *Times*.

At the advice of Clarence Darrow, on December 5 the accused men entered pleas of guilty. "Work of William J. Burns," said Assistant District Attorney Joe Ford, "drove them to confession as a means of escaping the extreme penalty." Clarence Darrow was twice indicted on separate charges of bribing jurors; when he promised never to plead another case in California the matter was dropped. Intermittently in the headlines for another three and one-half years, the story of violence came to an end when all men who had a part in the *Times* dynamiting were found and convicted.

By then, "William J. Burns" was virtually synonymous with "private detective." In the process of gaining international fame the detective who had voluntarily surrendered his badge brought respectability to a vocation suddenly made glamorous.

"Occident," owned by Leland Stanford; trotting at a 2.30 gait over the Sacramento track, in July, 1877
—A Muybridge photo copyrighted in 1877

Development of Motion Pictures Was Triggered by Wealthy Horse-Lover Leland Stanford

Leland Stanford won fame as governor of California, builder of the Central Pacific Railroad, and United States senator. Persons who knew him intimately agreed that more than any of those roles he liked that of breeder and trainer and racer of fine horses.

Most persons who spent time around stables and race tracks were interested only in an animal's bloodline and speed. Stanford, who had studied law and had no formal training in anatomy, was absorbed with the problem of how a horse runs. He called the movement "poetry in motion," but was unable to decide whether an animal moves at high speed by pulling with his forefeet or by pushing with his hind feet.

A long-established and widely circulated tradition, unsupported by documentary evidence but wholly plausible, holds that Stanford got

151

into a dicussion of the matter with James R. Keene and Frederick MacCrellish. Stanford, according to this tradition, ventured to suggest that "at some point in his gait, a trotter may actually have all four feet off the ground." Keene and MacCrellish are said to have scoffed so loudly at this preposterous notion that the railroad president offered to wager $25,000 that he was right—and was promptly taken on by the two doubters.

Regardless of whether or not that is the precise genesis of Stanford's otherwise hard to explain goal, he set out to prove himself correct by means of cameras. Hints and brief references in his letters and public statements indicate that he had fixed upon the idea as early as 1870. In order to test the camera's capacity to show how a horse runs, he needed an expert photographer.

Such a person reached California in 1872. Eadweard J. Muybridge, who had gained his experience and made his reputation in England, was one of the most noted photographers of the era. He agreed to try to see if he could get a shot of a horse with all four feet off the ground.

Photography was in its infancy, however, and no known equipment was capable of making an exposure in less than one-twelfth of a second. That time interval was much too great to freeze a racehorse in action. But in a period of only five years, equipment was developed that permitted an exposure of just one one-thousandth of a second. Muybridge had that equipment when he returned to California in 1877.

Leland Stanford's Palo Alto farm, located at the site of present-day Stanford University, had a fast track plus a promising stallion named Occident. It took only a few days for Muybridge to produce a still shot that baffled many veteran horsemen who shook their heads in disbelief when they saw Occident flying through the air with all four feet uplifted.

Not satisfied with having won his argument or his bet or both, Leland Stanford persuaded the English photographer to try to get photos showing every position in a horse's stride. It took a year and at least $40,000 to get all the equipment ready.

Early attempts to trip cameras by means of strings stretched across the race track failed. Stanford brought in John D. Isaacs, an amateur photographer and professional designer of railroads. Isaacs scrapped the use of strings designed to activate cameras when struck by a horse's leg, and went to what was ultra-sophisticated equipment for the era.

He placed a series of cameras at precise intervals along the track, then linked each with a cylinder equipped with pins arranged in spiral fashion. Elaborate electrical circuits made it possible for revolution of the cylinder to activate each camera in precise succession—one after another. Trial and error revealed that when cameras were properly spaced it was possible to get a dozen different photos of Occident during a single stride.

Not until many sequential sets of photos had been snapped did anyone involved in the experiment think of projecting such stills in rapid succession. Here it was clearly Muybridge the photographer and not Stanford the horse lover who conceived and executed the idea. Early in the fall of 1879 Muybridge gave a demonstration to guests who had come to the Stanford mansion. They exclaimed in awe as equipment whirred, twenty-four separate photos of Occident followed one another in rapid succession—and the horse appeared to be running.

Stanford's biographer, Norman E. Tutorow, terms that exhibition "the world's first home movie." It was, in fact, the first time in human experience that anyone—amateur or professional—had conveyed the impression of rapid movement by means of quick-moving still photos arranged in sequence for that purpose.

Leland Stanford footed the bill for publication of a then-expensive ($10) volume, chiefly photographic, about *The Horse in Motion*. Edited by J. D. B. Stillman, M.D., whose interest centered in the physiological aspects of racing, it evoked a suit for damages by Muybridge. He lost the case but the book did not sell. Most copies were purchased by Stanford, stored in his San Francisco mansion, and destroyed in the fire of 1906.

Though the book was a commercial failure, it had a profound impact. Muybridge became a sought-after notable on the international lecture circuit—expected, of course, to show a few seconds of Occident's running by means of what the photographer called his "zoogyroscope."

In Europe and in America scientists and inventors set out to transform the zoogyroscope from a toy into a new tool with which to feed visual information to viewers. One of those most interested was Thomas Alva Edison. He made important contributions to the developing art, others added their refinements and innovations, and the motion picture came into being. Edison's interest was so keen that he actually produced talking motion pictures, of a sort, about 1913—more than a

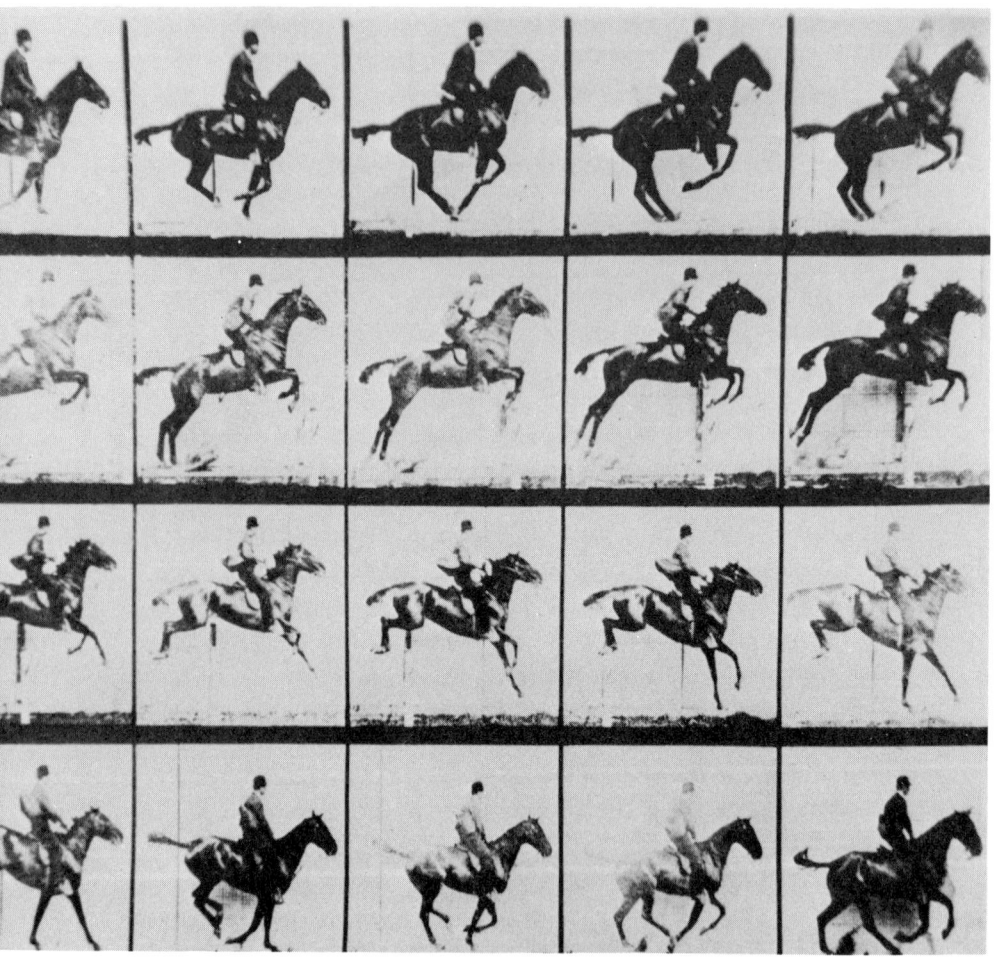

Many Muybridge photos—not just one—showed Leland Stanford's racer with all four feet off the ground simultaneously. (Sequence here is not identical with that of Muybridge's original photos)

decade before an unplanned variation from a Warner Bros. script produced the first commercial talkie.

Not even tradition gives any hint as to whether or not Leland Stanford ever collected $25,000 from James R. Keene and Frederick MacCrellish. But every careful survey of the birth and infancy of motion pictures includes at least a footnote acknowledging that the curiosity of a wealthy horse lover triggered their development.

Caned inside the Senate chamber, Sumner was permanently crippled by Brooks of South Carolina

High Jinks on Capitol Hill Contribute to Low Ratings for Our Lawmakers

Congressmen and Senators, makers of laws and shapers of the nation, have often flouted prevailing standards of conduct. Sometimes they have deliberately broken the law. Highly publicized antics, often told and retold for decades, have contributed to low ratings for our lawmakers. Late in 1981 the Gallup Poll asked Americans to rate 24 professions and occupations for honesty and ethical standards. Senators came in 14th, just below stockbrokers. Congressmen finished a low 17th, a trifle above realtors.

John C. Calhoun of South Carolina broke no law by his engineering of a "gag rule" in 1835. But he effectively thumbed his nose at a large and growing body of public opinion. Under the bylaw the Senate adopted at Calhoun's insistence, every resolution concerning slavery was automatically "laid upon the table" without discussion.

William J. Graves, representing Kentucky in Congress, did break the law. When a verbal exchange erupted over the Calhoun gag rule, Graves challenged Jonathan Cilley of New Hampshire to a duel. The lawmakers met at famous Bladensburg duelling field on February 24, 1838, and exchanged two shots with deer rifles. Though wounded, with his third shot the Kentuckian supposed to exemplify law and order killed the lawmaker who had differed with him.

Stephen A. Douglas of Illinois pulled a fast one with the blessing of President Pierce. In 1854 he moved that the Territory of Nebraska be established "with or without slavery, as its citizens might later decide." It was debate over the ensuing slippery Kansas-Nebraska Bill that brought back into the political arena a one-term Congressman from Illinois, Abe Lincoln.

Twenty years later senators and representatives voted themselves salary raises of $5,000 to $7,000. But they didn't do it openly. Instead they tacked an amendment to a general appropriation bill. Ostensibly designed to boost Ulysses S. Grant's salary from $25,000 to $50,000 a year, the "Salary Grab Bill" that fooled few taxpayers passed the House by 102 to 96 and the Senate by 36 to 27. Once established, that back door approach to raiding the U. S. Treasury has since been used in numerous variations.

As a technique for thwarting majority opinion, the filibuster is as legal as a salary grab—and just as devious. Huey Long of Louisiana spoke for 15½ hours attacking the National Recovery Act of 1935. Senator Wayne Morse of Oregon topped that performance in April 1953 by talking continuously for 22 hours and 26 minutes in an attempt to prevent passage of the 1953 Tidelands Oil Bill. Four years later, Senator Strom Thurmond of South Carolina moved his mouth continuously for 24 hours and 19 minutes in a ploy designed to stall the Civil Rights Bill of 1957. By doing so, he topped the previous record set in 1953.

Representative Laurence M. Keitt of South Carolina didn't have much to say. He just called Galusha Grow of Pennsylvania "a Republican black puppy" before hitting him on the jaw and knocking him cold. With regional tensions mounting on the eve of the Civil War,

Congressman Sam Houston, tried by his peers, was found guilty and was given a mild reprimand

many lawmakers had brought weapons with them. Throughout the chamber, knives and pistols flashed and it appeared that a general melee would break out on the floor of the House. Someone sent a huge earthenware spittoon crashing toward a foe; so many men stopped to

John C. Calhoun engineered a "gag rule" that was perfectly legal, but which thwarted the will of the American people

wipe off spray that the fight fizzled to an end.

No blows were exchanged between Senator George F. Hoar of Massachusetts and Senator Lucius Quintus Cincinnatus Lamar in 1879. But the Mississippi lawmaker with a name that seemed to come straight from Roman history roared with rage as a prelude to a personal attack. Using language for which schoolboys would have been sent to the principal's office, Lamar castigated his colleague as being "Not an Eagle, but a Vulture."

Tennessee Congressman Sam Houston took an Indian woman as his common-law wife and accepted adoption into the Cherokee Nation. Using language much milder than that of Lamar, Stanberry of Ohio sneered at Houston, who waited until adjournment, then pounced on his foe and gave him a thorough thrashing. Indignation ran high; perennially-drunk Houston was put on trial by his peers. He got off with a reprimand. Later, as President of the Republic of Texas, he said that "If I had been tried before an ordinary tribunal instead of the Congress, my name would today be forgotten and I would still be a drunken squaw-man."

Senator Charles Sumner of Massachusetts insulted the state of South Carolina in general, and her lawmakers in particular. Preston Brooks, congressman from the Palmetto State, considered challenging Sumner to a duel. He abandoned the idea because he felt Sumner's acceptance would have made him Brooks' social equal. In May, 1856, Brooks entered the Senate chamber carrying a gold-headed cane. He flailed Sumner into unconsciousness and was fined $300. Indignation over permanent injuries to Sumner led Brooks to resign his seat in Congress, but it was three years before the crippled Senator Sumner could return to his place on Capitol Hill.

Brooks was a conspicuous exception. Few lawmakers who have wantonly broken the law or the spirit of the law by their conduct in our nation's most powerful lawmaking body have received any punishment at all. But voters tend to remember. That's one reason the Gallup Poll found druggists, dentists, doctors, engineers, college teachers, clergy, police officers, bankers, TV commentators, newspaper reporters, funeral directors and stockbrokers ranking above congressmen and senators in a survey of opinions about honesty and ethical standards.

Mark Twain read no findings from public opinion polls. He simply put into memorable words what multitudes of ordinary voters had already come to accept: "There is no distinctive American criminal class—except the Congress."

Marble bust of Pope Gregory XIII

Some Confusion Still Remains from the Shortest Year in American History

Citizens of Philadelphia, Boston, New York, Richmond, Charleston and points between went to bed on September 2, 1752. Next morning when they got up, it was September 14.

Today the annual pattern of one-hour changes between standard and daylight saving time creates confusion. No wonder there was chaos plus anger in the year when 11 days were dropped from the calendar.

Every time George Washington's birthday is celebrated, calendar havoc is still evident. Most history and reference books say that he was born on February 22, 1732. But some important biographies are at pains to point out that he was born on February 11, 1731.

AMERICA'S SHORTEST YEAR

Which are right?

Strangely, both!

Because the earth's annual revolution around the sun doesn't occur in an exact number of whole days, the calendar has often gotten out of kilter.

Julius Caesar, who was far from the first to grapple with problems of the calendar, made important reforms in 46 B.C. His system, the Julian (or Old Style) calendar, treats the year as consisting of 365¼ days. Close, but not close enough. An error of 11 minutes per year becomes significant when it accumulates for centuries.

Churchmen were especially concerned because the date of Easter is pegged to the date of the vernal equinox. Traditionally registered on March 21, it came on March 11 in 1545, when the famous Council of Trent met.

At the request of concerned leaders, Pope Sixtus IV invited a noted astronomer to "reconstruct the calendar." Before the job was finished the scientist died suddenly. So Pope Gregory XIII took up the calendar issue shortly after becoming pontiff in 1572. He spent a decade consulting Europe's leading astronomers and mathematicians. Finally, with their help, he adopted a new formula.

On March 1, 1582, Gregory issued a long bull establishing a new calendar. Today it is known as the Gregorian (or New Style) calendar. In order to restore the vernal equinox to March 21, it was directed that "the day following October 5 shall be reckoned as the 15th of that month."

Catholic nations generally accepted the dictum of the pope, though there were mass protests in some regions. In most non-Catholic countries, both rulers and common folk balked at the notion of adopting what they called "a popish calendar."

Scotland capitulated in 1600. Protestant states of Germany followed in 1700, along with Denmark and Sweden. Fiercely anti-Catholic Britain held out against all change and stuck to the Julian calendar. King George I, born in Hanover in 1660, didn't want "the old ways" modified. He clung so tenaciously to tradition that he paid a ceremonial visit to a battlefield — making him the last English ruler to risk his life in war.

French and Spanish colonies in the New World adopted the Gregorian calendar. But in North America, all British colonies followed the example of their king and clung to the Julian.

Some Europeans protested Gregory's formula but ended by adopting it

By the time George II became ruler of Britain in 1727, the error in the Julian calendar had mounted to 11 days. With the king's consent the Earl of Chesterfield introduced a bill into Parliament. Under its terms Britain and all her colonies would switch to the Gregorian calendar in 1752. After long debate the calendar reform became law. One of its provisions stipulated that "after the 2nd day of September in 1752, the next ensuing day shall be held as the 14th."

There were protests throughout the English-speaking world. Many colonial voices were vigorous and loud. A not-so-obscure American named George Washington fumed at the notion of celebrating his birthday on February 22, instead of on February 11.

Creditors were required to make allowance for the lost 11 days, but few complied with the edict. Hence debtors who paid interest by the year paid for 365 days but got only 354 days' use of the money. "Give us back our 11 days!" became a popular slogan.

Protestors wasted their energy. Enforced by the king and his officers, the calendar change reduced the annual error to about 25 seconds. At the same time the observance of New Year's Day was shifted from late March to January 1. That meant, for three months of the year, a difference of 1 year plus 11 days between Old Style and New Style systems.

George Washington really was born on February 11, 1731 (Old Style). When he toured the South in 1791, he observed with satisfaction that in this section of the nation many citizens still celebrated his birthday on February 11th. Yet not even the man who fought calendar change almost as stubbornly as he fought the British could prevail against the more accurate Gregorian system.

Now universally used, the Catholic-rooted new way of reckoning time requires that dates prior to September 14, 1752, be brought into harmony with it. That means subtraction of 1 year plus 11 days from every date in the period, say, 1732–1752, for the first three months of each year, only. For the balance of each year, the 11-day change is adequate.

In practice, many early American documents are corrected only for especially important dates. When reprinted for use in schools, such documents may include some Old Style dates and some New Style dates. An 11-day difference becomes important only when events of a period are treated chronologically. But even when dealing with things that happened 250 years ago (in January, February, or March), a year plus 11 days may be significant. Small wonder that some confusion still remains with us from the shortest year in our history.

The Rev. John Wesley, M.A., founder of Methodism

A Girl of 18 Played a Crucial Role in the Start of a Worldwide Religious Movement

Like nearly everyone in Savannah, Sophy Hopkey was eager for a look at the colony's newly arrived missionary. So she was one of 20 persons present when The Reverend John Wesley, M.A., first administered Holy Communion in Georgia. Neither she nor Wesley ever forget the date: Saturday, March 13, 1736. How very, very well Sophy did remember . . .

One of the few eligible females in Oglethorpe's infant colony, the girl of 18 wasn't bothered by the clergyman's short stature or his face that was already stern at 33. To her he symbolized all that was exciting and romantic about faraway England . . . and Oxford University . . . and the Church of England . . . Within weeks Sophy put timidity aside and accosted Oglethorpe himself. Responding to her questions, the colony's founder said he thought Mr. Wesley would like her best in white—the color symbolizing purity.

That's why Sophy wore white when she attended early morning prayers at Wesley's house, then remained to eat breakfast with him and a colleague. Soon she was present (radiant in pure white) at evening prayers, too. When she said she'd like to learn French, linguist Wesley graciously offered to spend an hour a day teaching her.

He had come to Georgia in order to convert Indians to Christianity—but except for aging Chief Tomo-chi-chi the missionary seldom saw a native American. As chaplain to the colony, it seemed fitting that he inconvenience himself a bit for a girl who was often "the most affected of his listeners." Besides, her aunt was married to Thomas Causton, who was the colony's chief magistrate and public storekeeper.

Every morning Wesley rose at four o'clock in order to pray and to search the Scriptures. After at least an hour of soul-searching he was ready to face the challenges of the day. But nearly every hour he stopped for 5 or 10 minutes of renewed prayer—then carefully recorded in his diary the time devoted to that exercise. Wednesdays and Fridays were days of fasting and penance.

Soon his fast-expanding diary (written in a code he had devised) began including more and longer references to Miss Sophy. He confessed himself frightened to realize that not all of his thoughts were directed to the salvation of his own soul and to the spiritual welfare of his flock. To make things worse, he was positive that Miss Sophy showed every sign of being interested in him as a male as well as a pastor.

Their relationship grew more intimate . . . and Wesley's notations in his diary grew more tortured. They spent 5 or 6 days and nights together, travelling by boat the 100 miles from Frederica to Savannah. In bad weather they slept crowded together with the crew of 4 and the lone other passenger, all covered with sails to keep the water off them. Wesley entertained Sophy by reading to her—from Patrick's "Prayers" and Fleury's "History of the Church."

Back in Savannah, his diary entry for December 19, 1736, included entries exhorting himself "in the name of God, to be more watchful, before and in prayer; not to touch even her clothes by choice; think

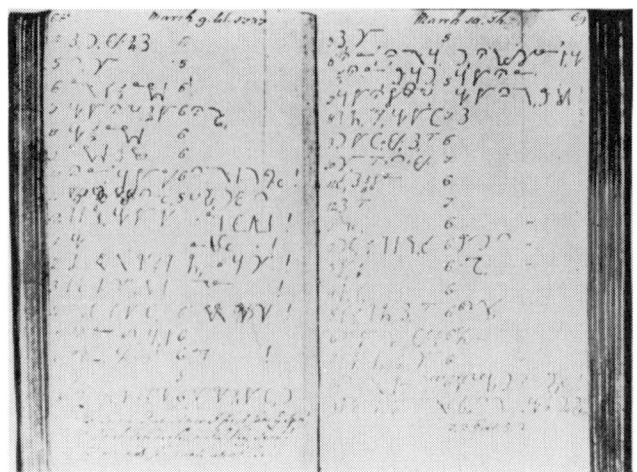

Wesley's diary in code he developed; March 9–10, 1737

not of her." He wasted his ink; he couldn't get Sophy out of his mind even in hours of fasting and penance. Nor could he forget that Masters Tom Mellichamp and William Williamson had shown clear and not 100% holy interest in the girl. Perhaps he should warn her . . .

Events of 1737, had they not been so fateful in their long-range impact, would seem like real-life scenes in a comic opera.

Over and over Wesley was on the brink of urging the marriage that, deep down, he was sure Sophy eagerly desired. Always though he hesitated and stopped just one short step away from the fateful moment that would permit no turning back. Often perplexed and sometimes annoyed, the girl made it clear that if Wesley didn't act soon it would be too late.

He consulted a group of Moravian friends, and was told that it would be best for him to give up the idea of marriage. Less than fully convinced, he cast lots in order to seek the will of God—and of 3 alternatives drew the slip that told him: "Think of it no more." He couldn't drive her from his mind but he could not bring himself to ask for her hand. With the anniversary of their meeting almost at hand, Sophy told her aunt to announce her engagement to William Williamson. They were married on Saturday, March 12, 1737—exactly one year from the day Sophy Hopkey and John Wesley first saw one another.

Mrs. Williamson, still a member of Wesley's parish, was first warned and then admonished to be more zealous about "owning her fault and declaring her repentance" for lack of spiritual discipline. She ignored her pastor's exhortations. One month later he refused to admit her to the altar at a service of Holy Communion.

On the following day (August 8, 1737) Pastor Wesley was shocked when served with a warrant charging him with "defaming said Sophia" and asking damages in the amount of £1,000. Magistrate Thomas Causton visited the rectory to confront Wesley with more charges. A Grand Jury of 44 males overwhelmingly voted a lengthy True Bill against the pastor.

Matters went from bad to worse. Unable to get a formal trial started, Wesley announced his plans to leave. A new court order commanded him to stay and to post surety of £50. So the man who had come as a missionary fled in the night as "a prisoner at large."

Back in England the Oxford University scholar who had as a student founded a Holy Club was under no delusions. He was a total failure—a disgrace to his God and himself. Eternally at his prayers and soul-searching, "of all men most tormented," he went ("most unwillingly") to a prayer meeting in Aldersgate Street, London. There a profound religious experience made him into an evangelist.

Numerous Methodist bodies and even more non-Methodist ones with Wesleyan theology sprang up as a result of his influence. Worldwide an estimated 30 million persons are adherents of churches shaped by John Wesley's life and thought. Suppose Sophy Hopkey had been a trifle more patient—or a bit more persuasive? Had she become the bride of the priest nearly twice her age, disappointment, disgrace, and discovery born of desperation wouldn't have pushed Wesley into starting a new religious movement.

Artists' conception of Wesley and companions fleeing from Georgia

Congressman Lincoln favored gradual emancipation, and President Lincoln took the same position

Publication of the Emancipation Proclamation Was Psychological Warfare at Its Earliest and Best

January 1, 1863, saw publication of an edict that changed American life forever. Aimed at what is now the Southeast, it is today hailed throughout the world as a triumph of compassionate statesmanship. Yet when issued, the Emancipation Proclamation was a desperate military gamble made by a man not wearing a uniform.

Often regarded with nostalgia as a homespun and perhaps naive country lawyer, Abraham Lincoln was actually more like a 19th-century prototype of courtroom wizard F. Lee Bailey. He took on a great variety of cases that sometimes involved large sums of money, and usually managed to trounce his opposition. Lawyer Lincoln sometimes worked for defendants, sometimes counseled the prosecution.

When he reached the nation's capital, Congressman Lincoln was asked to declare his view of the red-hot issue of the day: total abolition of slavery. He took a middle-of-the-road stance in which he favored emancipation, but preferred that it should be achieved gradually.

As President of the United States he adhered to that early set of views. But once he was in the White House the man who capitalized upon having been born in a log cabin was catapaulted into a role he didn't fully understand in advance. "Honest Abe" was inaugurated as our 16th president on March 4, 1861. On the same day he became commander in chief of the military forces of the United States.

Much of his first full day in office, March 5, was spent conferring with military leaders. General Winfield Scott, who earlier opposed withdrawal from Ft. Sumter, now advocated evacuation of the base located in Charleston harbor. His change of mind came too late. When the first shots were fired at Ft. Sumter on April 12, Lincoln the commander in chief had no choice; he was forced to take an active role in the Civil War.

Lincoln, the war-time president, is fairly well known. Lincoln, the commander in chief, is virtually unknown today.

That certainly was not the case during the early 1860's. No one north or south of the battle lines was left wondering who made the final decisions in Washington. That applied not only to the incredibly radical and daring Emancipation Proclamation, but also to varied vital issues not so vividly remembered now.

How much freedom should a war-time citizen have?

Prodded by Winfield Scott, whose judgment was especially respected, the commander in chief issued a terse order on April 27, 1862. Under its terms the federal blockade was at once to be extended to the coasts of Virginia and North Carolina. Simultaneously, "for reasons of public safety," the treasured privilege of *habeas corpus* was suspended along a line running from Washington to Philadelphia.

Many in the North angrily questioned Lincoln's right to order persons held in jail without explanation or recourse. But Congress was not in session. No other agency or person had any power to do more than protest without effect.

So for a nearly-forgotten period of 11 weeks Abraham Lincoln was military dictator of the Union. All major decisions were executive ones from which there was no appeal. Ignoring Congressional limits upon spending, the commander in chief called for volunteers to enlarge the army with speed. All telegraphic communications originating in Washington were censored. Martial law in many regions permitted arrest and confinement of a suspect without showing cause.

A mounting storm of protest within the Union included serious talk of impeachment proceedings. After 80 days the April order was lifted, but *habeas corpus* privileges were suspended at least 7 other times by Lincoln or by military commanders who acted with his consent.

What new weapons should be tried on the battlefield?

Commander in Chief Lincoln kept in close personal touch with experiments and inventions designed to increase Union firepower. Always the White House was open to any inventor who came along offering a new kind of gun. Once the president was nearly killed when a rocket blew up in a demonstration firing.

Professional military men tended to rely upon proved and tested weapons. Against their resistance, the man who has become the stereo-

Closing lines of the proclamation, with Lincoln's signature witnessed by Seward

Major General David Hunter's emancipation was countermanded

Lt. General Winfield Scott, onetime candidate for the presidency

type of compassion backed the trial and use of both the breech-loading rifle and the new-fangled rapid-fire Gatling gun.

What official stance should the United States take toward slavery in all its forms, wherever it might be practiced?

Major General John C. Fremont, born in Georgia and reared in South Carolina, had been a political opponent of Congressman Lincoln. In 1856 Fremont easily defeated the Illinois lawmaker in a contest for the Republican nomination for the presidency. In August, 1861, General Fremont declared martial law after smashing Confederate forces in Missouri. One clause of his proclamation gave freedom to slaves of the state. Lincoln requested his general to withdraw the order; Fremont refused. So Commander in Chief Lincoln then ordered his subordinate to rescind his edict of emancipation; Fremont had no choice—he obeyed.

At Hilton Head, South Carolina, General David Hunter ordered emancipation of slaves on May 9, 1862. His edict applied only to the states of Florida, Georgia, and South Carolina. Yet just 10 days after it was issued, it was repudiated by his commander in chief.

By then, most Union leaders agreed that gradual emancipation would have little or no effect upon the war. Only a quick and dramatic move would have an effect upon world opinion. But too quick a set of actions might lose their force if taken during a period of Confederate battlefield victories. And too drastic a set of actions would trigger near-revolt among slave owners in Union territory.

An emancipation proclamation was drafted during the summer. At the insistence of William H. Seward, Secretary of State, it was held until the Union could rejoice at events on some battlefield. September, 1862, brought exultation at having turned back the Confederates at Antietam. So Lincoln gave states "then in rebellion" 100 days (until January 1, 1863) to return to the Union. He warned that he would then issue another proclamation "whereby the slaves in those states [still in rebellion] will become forever free."

Many in the north castigated their commander in chief for having gone too far, too fast. Fiery abolitionists like Horace Greeley and John C. Fremont berated him for not going far enough or fast enough. For the New Year's Day proclamation applied only to states in armed rebellion. It left slavery untouched in West Virginia, Tennessee, Maryland, Missouri, Delaware, Kentucky, and specified counties of Louisiana and Virginia. It did nothing about voting rights in the north, where the handful of states that permitted blacks to vote had created a maze of barriers. The hated "$3/5$th rule" under which a black was counted as 60% of a person for purposes of Congressional representation—in the north as well as in the south—was untouched.

Perhaps the military decision by the commander in chief did all that could have been achieved at the time. It triggered no immediate sweeping changes in patterns of life anywhere. It did set in motion irresistable forces that long afterward led to legal equality for all male Americans.

In 1863 the instant and transforming impact of the Emancipation Proclamation was upon attitudes. For to a degree then unequalled, and seldom if ever matched in later generations, Lincoln's dramatic statement constituted a bold act of psychological warfare. Without firing a shot the rail-splitter president boosted the morale of the Union. At the same time he raised fearful questions within the Confederacy and riveted the eyes of the world upon those who fought for the Union and for the abolition of slavery.

Thomas Nast communicated with voters who didn't read English through the medium of art

A Cartoonist's Pen Helped to Topple a Political Empire

Citizens of New York in the era after the Civil War referred to William Marcy Tweed by just one word: Boss. As chairman of the Tammany General Committee, he actually was boss of the city's Democratic organization. Tweed and associates used faked leases, padded bills, false vouchers and other devices to plunder the city of a sum estimated to range between 30 and 200 million dollars.

Lawyer-reformer Samuel J. Tilden attacked Tweed and his ring fiercely, but with little effect. German-born cartoonist Thomas Nast used his pen to help to topple what many analysts consider to have been America's most powerful and most crooked political empire.

Harper's Weekly *cartoon that led to recognition and capture of the fugitive*

New York had a large population of voters who did not speak or read English. Cartoons by Nast reached these persons, when editorials and public speeches did not. Tweed himself once remarked that "even if the voters can't read, they can look at the damned pictures." An early one that particularly infuriated him depicted the Boss with a dollar mark for a face.

After years of crusading on the part of Thomas Nast and others,

Tweed was brought to trial on charges of forgery and larceny. Judge Noah Davis presided over proceedings that began on January 7, 1873. Largely as a result of the impact of scores of hard-hitting cartoons, public opinion no longer supported the political boss. He was convicted, fined $12,750, and sentenced to spend 12 years in the county penitentiary on Blackwell's island. An appeal to a higher court led to reduction of the sentence to a $250 fine plus one year in prison.

No words were needed to convey a powerful message

While Tweed was behind bars, still manipulating his political machine and still derided by Nast cartoons, the New York Legislature enacted new statutes. Under their terms it was possible, for the first time, for the state to bring suit to recover money stolen from the public treasury.

Released on January 15, 1875, Boss Tweed was immediately made a defendant in a civil suit and hence was rearrested. Prosecutors hoped to trace and to recover as much as 6 million dollars—a small fraction of the total believed to have been stolen from the public by Tweed and his allies.

Bail was set at 3 million dollars in cash or 6 million dollars in real estate. He refused to post bail, so was confined to Ludlow Street jail— the debtor's prison of the era.

Boss Tweed escaped (perhaps with the assistance of jail keepers) on December 4, 1875. He went into hiding for a few months. Then he assembled all the cash he could and slowly worked his way to Cuba.

Meanwhile Samuel J. Tilden had received the Democratic nomination for the presidency. During the week that followed his June nomination, Thomas Nast published a new and hard-hitting cartoon in *Harper's Weekly,* one of the most widely circulated periodicals of the era. Though the cartoon was directed against candidate Tilden, it featured Nast's old enemy, Boss Tweed.

As he often did, Nast this time drew the face more like a portrait than a caricature. He depicted a figure in the striped suit of a convict, with the face of Tweed, who held two children by their collars while he pointed to a political billboard. If Tweed saw the cartoon, it made no difference to him. He had already arranged to take passage on the brig *Carmen,* bound for Vigo, Spain. He chose that destination because Spain then had no extradition treaty with the United States.

While Tweed's ship was on the ocean a Spanish subscriber to *Harper's Weekly* saw the Nast cartoon at his home in Madrid. Don Benigno S. Suarez selected Vigo as Tweed's most likely port of entry, so sent the cartoon to police there.

When the *Carmen* docked, authorities were waiting. Unable to read English, from study of the cartoon they had concluded that Tweed was a kidnapper. Though disguised as a common sailor and busy scrubbing a deck, the one-time Boss was immediately recognized and arrested.

Tweed was briefly jailed in Vigo. Then the man who seemed to

Tweed, the manipulator, is busy even in jail

the Spanish to look as though he stole little boys was released to the commander of the U. S. warship *Franklin*. Now legally in default of a 6 million dollar judgment, he was returned to New York in November, 1876.

After a few months he was offered his freedom in exchange for turning state's evidence and surrendering all of his assets. While talks proceeded the prisoner fell ill. At high noon on April 12, 1878, Boss Tweed died in Ludlow Street jail—having been toppled from power and then brought to justice by the power of a cartoonist's pen.

Portrait of John Paul Jones, as issued by French engraver J.M. Moreau

Revolutionary Hero John Paul Jones Took the War to Britain and Brought Panic to Persons 3,000 Miles from the American Colonies

Fifth child of a Scottish market gardener, John Paul Jones had only a smattering of formal schooling. He was apprenticed to a merchant of Whitehaven, who took him to the American colonies at age 13. When his master's business failed, the boy served for 2 years as a midshipman in the British Royal Navy. When the Continental Congress created a small navy, Jones won appointment as a first lieutenant.

Serving on the cruiser *Alfred,* Lieutenant John Paul Jones hoisted the first flag ever to float above an American warship. The yellow silk banner first displayed in January, 1776, bore the figure of a rattlesnake. Eighteen months later the native of Scotland was given command of the 18-gun *Ranger* — first American warship to fly the new national flag of stars and stripes.

Sailing from Portsmouth, New Hampshire, on November 1, 1777, the *Ranger* carried papers that gave her authority to rove the seas in search of British vessels. Jones took his ship across the Atlantic and anchored in French waters. From the U. S. Commissioners to France, of whom Benjamin Franklin was one, he got new orders. Probably at his request, language of the document was deliberately vague.

Already, he had conceived one of the most daring plans in the annals of the sea. He had decided to raid British ports and to lead his men in an invasion of the island kingdom whose mercenary soldiers were making war upon American patriots.

"I resolved," he wrote in one of his lengthy letters, "to make the greatest efforts to bring to an end the barbarous ravages to which the English turned in America. I had received no order at all to avenge these injuries, and I had not at all communicated my plans to the American Commission at Paris." That is, he was acting largely upon his own.

April, 1778, saw his plan put into action. With a party of volunteers he rowed into Whitehaven harbor, with which he was familiar from boyhood. Americans managed to spike at least 30 of the big guns in the fort. Then, using tar as fuel, they set the 400-ton merchant vessel *Thomson* on fire.

Damage was not on a large scale — perhaps £4,500. But in the words of the invader, "What was done is sufficient to show that not all their boasted navy can protect their own coasts; and that the scenes of distress which they have occasioned in America may be soon brought home to their own door."

Historian Lincoln Lorenz echoes the verdict of the daredevil seaman. "Psychologically the victory was Jones'," he writes; "morally also it was his."

British newspapers literally exploded with reports plus rumors. Seaport towns organized for defense. Ordinary folk of Britain, some of whom had thought little of a war being fought 3,000 miles away, suddenly found it at their doorsteps. For the foray into Whitehaven harbor really meant that Americans might strike another blow, anywhere along the coast of Britain, at any time.

A second attack was launched on April 23, 1778. This time, Jones and members of his crew landed at St. Mary's Isle—famous as the residence of one of England's most prominent families.

Invaders hoped to capture the Earl of Selkirk in order to offer him in exchange for Americans who were being held prisoner by the British. Unfortunately for the raiders, the nobleman was away from home. Though Lady Helen, wife of the earl, would have served well as a hostage, Jones refused to take her. He did permit his men to ransack the mansion and to make off with the silver plate they found in it. Years later, the gallant American purchased the silver with part of his own prize money and returned it to Lady Selkirk.

Again, newspapers of Britain were filled with dispatches about the man whom some called John the Painter [panther]. Readers of the *Morning Chronicle and London Advertiser* were astonished to be told that "The audacious conduct of the crew of the American privateer will have this good effect: it will teach our men of war on the coast stations, and our cruisers in St. George's channel, to keep a more sharp lookout."

Many national leaders were by now thoroughly alarmed. But among ordinary folk, the man who had dared to defy the world's mightiest navy was sometimes treated as a Robin Hood of the sea. He

Flying from the **Ranger,** *the Stars and Stripes gets from a French squadron the very first salute given it by Europeans*

British cruise of the **Ranger**

became the subject of numerous Scottish and English ballads, some of which were wholly complimentary.

Just one day after his second foray upon British soil, Jones sailed into waters off Belfast and spotted the warship H.M.S. *Drake*. In a letter dated May 8, 1778, he emphasized his knowledge that the British vessel had more men than his own, plus greater fire power. But as he described the ensuing conflict:

"The Ships met, and the advantage was disputed with great fortitude on each side for an Hour and Five minutes, when the gallant Commander of the *Drake* fell, and Victory was declared in favor of the *Ranger*. His amiable Lieutenant lay mortally wounded besides near forty of the inferior officers and crew killed and wounded. I buried them in a spacious grave, with the Honors due to the memory of the brave."

The British Admiralty responded with vigor. H.M.S. *Stag* and H.M.S. *Doctor* had already been ordered to pursue and to capture the invader. Now the 36-gun frigate *Thetis* plus the sloop of war *Heart of Oak* and the 32-gun *Boston* joined the chase, along with assorted smaller ships. Jones slipped through the net that had been drawn for him and on May 8 led the captured *Drake* into the harbor at Brest, France.

In a cruise of just 28 days the American naval hero had twice raided the coast of Britain. He had captured two merchant ships and destroyed others. Best of all, he had overpowered a man-of-war bigger and stronger than his own vessel.

News of his exploits electrified France — always at odds with Britain and presently struggling to decide how much help they dared to give to the Americans. Benjamin Franklin wrote jubilant letters home. Eventually the more than 200 prisoners taken by Jones were exchanged for Americans earlier captured by the British.

John Paul Jones is best remembered in present-day America for the famous battle in which his ship, the *Bonhomme Richard,* defeated the *Serapis*. In much of England, especially along the coasts, he is most vividly remembered because of the innumerable newspaper accounts and occasional ballads describing how he took the Revolutionary War to British soil.

Irish-Born William Paterson Triggered Creation of the U.S. Senate—and a Congressional Double Dividend for New Jersey

Born in County Antrim, Ireland, late in 1745, William Paterson was just five feet two inches tall and described as weighing just 120 pounds when "soaking wet." What he lacked in size the diminutive college-trained lawyer made up in tenacity. As an influential delegate to the Federal (or "Constitutional") Convention that determined the structure of the U.S. government, Paterson was outvoted when he presented a plan merely to modify the Articles of Confederation. But the "great compromise" triggered by that plan led to creation of the U.S. Senate and—eventually—to grossly disproportionate influence of New Jersey in Congress.

Delegates—seventy-four of them—had been named to convene in Philadelphia in the spring of 1787. Only fifty-four of them ever reached the City of Brotherly Love; when they set out from home only a handful (perhaps one in ten) expected the convention to frame a document such as the Constitution that eventually emerged from their debate.

From the beginning, it was clear that several issues would split the convention down the middle and that one—representation by states in a federal law-making body—might well prevent the establishment of a lasting union among former British colonies.

A handful of big and wealthy states, feared representatives of small and poor states, were likely to become all-powerful. If that was not the goal of the Virginia Resolves presented by the Commonwealth's Governor Edmund Randolph, it clearly would have been the effect of adoption of those resolutions. For Virginia (backed by Pennsylvania and by Massachusetts) boldly proposed a national legislature of two houses. According to the plan, the lower house would be elected by the people on the basis of state population—and the upper house would be selected by the lower. Adoption of the plan would have had the effect of placing the reins of government in the hands of lawmakers elected from the three big states.

Delegates debated the Virginia Resolves for four hot and increasingly acrimonious weeks. Acting as a committee of the whole, the convention voted on June 11 to establish proportional representation for the upper as well as the lower house of the legislative body that was to be created. It looked as though the influence of small states would be very small, indeed.

But when the convention reassembled on June 14 diminutive William Paterson, speaking with great fervor, requested adjournment until the next day. The delay, he explained, would enable the completion of a "purely federal" plan of government. When presented to delegates on the 15th it proved to be a revision of the Articles of Confederation under which every state, however small, retained much of its sovereignty.

Even the most ardent advocates of a system that would "prevent small states from being enslaved by large ones" privately conceded that the Paterson Plan never had a chance. But it might have the effect of blocking adoption of the Randolph Plan drawn up by the Virginia bloc—and forcing dissolution of the convention without any decisive action.

Referred to the committee of the whole, the diametrically-opposed plans were debated to the point of weariness and frustration. Finally, on July 16, Roger Sherman of Connecticut rose to propose a plan that became famous as "the great compromise." Let state representation in the lower house of Congress be determined by population, he suggested. But in the upper house permit the smallest state to be equal to the largest by giving every state two senators.

James Wilson of Pennsylvania had spoken against the Paterson Plan with great fervor. "Shall New Jersey have the same right or council in the nation with Pennsylvania?" he demanded. "I say no! It is unjust—I never will confederate on this plan!" Paterson, equally firm, had put himself on record for all time: "I will never consent to the present system (the Virginia Resolves, as amended by the committee of the whole), and I shall make all the interest against it in the state which I represent that I can. Myself or my state will never submit to tyranny or despotism!"

Spokesmen for opposing plans—largely but not entirely influenced by the size of states from which they came—grudgingly conceded that Sherman's compromise seemed to offer some satisfaction to both factions. Under it, heavily populated states would dominate the House of Representatives—designed to have a decisive voice in taxation and other fiscal matters. But a Senate made up of two persons from each state would preserve the essential feature of the Paterson Plan—namely, "a legislative chamber in which the states would vote equally, without regard to population or wealth."

As a governmental structure, the Congress of the United States actually was something new under the sun. Large states could make their influence felt, but would be powerless against a coalition of senators from small states. But the requirement for joint approval of bills would mean that no band of senators pushing for special interests of small states could overpower the House of Representatives whose numbers would be determined on the basis of proportional representation.

Expediency and a mutual desire to achieve some sort of compromise, not legislative brilliance, won out in the end. As a concession to nearly half of the framers of the U.S. Constitution who favored the Paterson Plan over the Randolph Plan, the U.S. Senate was created. During just two centuries it came to be one of the world's most powerful legislative bodies.

As for William Paterson, the fiery proponent of the rights of small states became an associate justice of the U.S. Supreme Court (in an era when the court had not yet gained its present vast prestige and power). Paterson died in 1806, decades too early to know that eventually the U.S. legislative system would yield a double bonus to the state he so fervently represented in 1787.

Today, geographically tiny New Jersey is on equal footing in the U.S. Senate with vast states like Texas and California. At the same time, growth of urban population has given New Jersey more than ordinary clout in the House of Representatives. Alaska, Delaware,

Hawaii, Idaho, Maine, Nevada, North Dakota, Rhode Island, Utah, and Wyoming, *combined,* have one less voice in the House than does New Jersey with her fifteen representatives.

Ardent Jerseyman that he was, even William Paterson wouldn't have had the nerve to demand for his state such a role as it has been given by the unique U.S. mix of House-plus-Senate that makes up the Congress.

William Fred Allen, "father of Standard Time"

Railroader William F. Allen Developed Our System of Standard Time — over Governmental Objections

At 12:00 noon on November 18, 1883, operators of 78,000 miles of railroads adopted a system of standard time. Under it the nation was divided into 4 geographical belts, or zones. Though never modified except for minor details, the system didn't gain legal sanction until March 19, 1918. As a wartime measure, Congress finally passed a Standard Time Act that day.

Until the railroads acted to clear up confused schedules, "sun time" was used throughout the United States. That meant a different pattern prevailed in practically every city and town. Sometimes there were differences within cities: in Washington, D.C., the clock at the Lincoln Memorial was 7 seconds away from the clock at the Capitol. Illinois had at least 27 different local times. Adjoining Indiana had only 23, but in Wisconsin there were at least 38 competing systems.

So long as a person stayed within a few miles of home, use of local or "sun" time created few problems. But if one bought a ticket for a distant destination that was to be reached by rail, it was a different matter. Each railroad operated its entire system according to sun time at the home office, or terminal.

As a result a New York Central train that left the Manhattan terminal on schedule and followed the schedule exactly, arrived in Buffalo 15 minutes late by Buffalo time. A transcontinental railroad trip was a nightmare. During the 3,000-mile trip a drummer who prided himself on always having the right time had to set his stem-winding watch at least 20 times to make corrections for changes.

Railroad executives who met in St. Louis in 1872 to work out summer schedules ended by establishing a time-table convention. Someone would have to draw up a workable proposal before the idea of railroad time, "standard across the nation," could even be considered.

Railroad magnate Cornelius Vanderbilt or one of his subordinates is believed to have said that "Bill Allen is just the right man for the job." Allen worked as a surveyor before becoming assistant editor of the "Official Railway Guide" in 1872.

After 9 years of work "The Allen Plan" was presented to railroad heads in November, 1881. Instead of time patterns that differed as greatly as locomotives, the plan provided for four time zones in the United States. Railroaders everywhere praised the proposal and gave it formal sanction in October, 1883. Most major lines agreed to put it into effect at 12:00 noon on November 18, 1883.

Nonrailroaders, especially holders of public office, voiced loud and fervent objections. Mayor Dogberry of Bangor, Maine, vetoed an ordinance seeking to establish Eastern Standard Time. He called the measure unconstitutional and labelled it "an attempt to change the immutable laws of God Almighty." U. S. Attorney-General Benjamin H. Brewster issued a general order warning that "no agency of the federal government has a right to adopt railroad time unless and until it is authorized by Congress."

In Indianapolis, editors of the *Sentinel* thundered that: "The sun will be requested to rise and set by railroad time. The planets must, in the future, make their circuits by such timetables as railroad magnates arrange. People will have to marry by railroad time, and die by railroad time." Many ordinary folk agreed with that viewpoint, protesting that they preferred "to live and die according to God's time, not Vanderbilt's."

Railroaders themselves had some complicated problems to solve. A typical order, from the general superintendent of the Louisville & Nashville Railroad, directed that: "Should any train be caught between telegraph stations at 10:00 A.M. on November 18, it must stop for 18 minutes. Then watches are to be turned back to 10:00, after which trains may proceed with great caution to the first telegraph station. At that station, watches must be checked against the new standard time."

Once the new system of time was adopted by railroads, most members of the general public came to accept it and even to praise it. But it took Congress 34½ years to give legal sanction to our system of Standard Time.

William F. Allen was architect of a plan that affects the life of every American. Yet his name appears in few history books. Except for the system he devised, his only memorial was a simple bronze plaque that for many years hung on the wall of a waiting room in the old Union Station of Washington, D.C.

Index

Adams, Abigail, 15
Adams, John, 35, 36, 102
Adams, John Quincy, 102
Adams, Lewis, 141
Alexander, Clifford, 88
Alexander, George B., 147
Allen, William F., 187
Armstrong, Gen. Samuel C., 142
Arnold, Philip, 169-171
Arthur, Gen. Chester A., 26

Bacon, Edmund, 81
Baker, Dr. J.S., 43
Beall, J. Glenn, 24
Bellinghausen, Fabian G. von, 64
Benton, Thomas Hart, 122
Birney, James G., 122
Bixby, Horace, 90
Blaine, James G., 50-52
Bloomfield, Joseph, 111
Bradhurst, Samuel, 110
Bradley, Charles, 43
Bradley, Joseph P., 29
Bragg, Gen. Braxton, 86
Brooks, Preston, 159
Brown, Bedford, 67
Brown, Harold P., 106, 107
Brown, Mr., 90, 93
Bulloch, James D., 95
Burchard, Rev. Samuel D., 52
Burke, Edmund, 131, 134
Burns, William J., 146-150
Burr, Aaron, 109-111
Butler, Pierce, 110
Butterfield, Daniel, 98-100

Cabell, Joseph, 82
Calhoun, John C., 155
Campbell, George, 141
Carlos III, King, 78
Carr, Dabney, Jr., 82

Chamberlain, Gov. Daniel H., 26
Chandler, Zach, 26
Charles I, 58-60
Charles II, 60
Chase, Samuel, 36, 109-111
Chilton, R.H., 39
Church, John B., 110
Cilley, Jonathan, 156
Clay, Henry, 31-33
Clemens, Henry, 91, 93
Clemens, Samuel L., 89-92, 159
Cleveland, Grover, 49-52
Clinton, Sir Henry, 78
Cochran, W. Burke, 106
Coke, Thomas William, 132
Cooper, Dr. Charles, 110
Correa de Serra, Abbe, 15
Cranch, William, 32
Cromwell, Oliver, 58-60
Currier, Charles, 48
Currier, Nathaniel, 46, 47
Curtiss, Glenn H., 115, 116

Darrow, Clarence, 150
Davis, David, 29
Davis, Jefferson, 96
De Soto, Hernando, 117
Dickens, Charles, 102
Dixon, Jeremiah, 43
Dixwell, John, 60
Douglas, Stephen A., 156
Durston, Warden, 107

Early, Jubal, 21-24
Edison, Thomas Alva, 105-108, 153

Field, Ben, 138
Ford, Joe, 150
Fox, Charles James, 131, 134
Franklin, Benjamin, 16-20, 134

INDEX

Franklin, William, 16–20
Frémont, Gen. John C., 171–172

Galvez, Gov. Bernardo de, 78
Gardiner, David, 122
Gardiner, Julia, 121
George III, King, 17, 77, 132
Germain, Lord George, 78
Gilmer, Thomas W., 122
Gist (or Guess), Nathaniel, 118
Gladstone, William, 30
Goffe, William, 60
Gompers, Samuel, 148
Grant, U.S., 26, 95, 140
Graves, William J., 156

Halpin, Maria, 51
Hamilton, Alexander, 11–12, 14, 109–110
Hamilton, Philip, 110
Hampton, Wade, 27
Harrison, William H., 31, 102, 104
Hart, John. *See* Kemmler, Willie
Hayes, Rutherford B., 25, 28, 29
Hill, Gen. D.H., 87
Holbrook, Stewart, 139
Holmes, Oliver Wendell, Jr., 24
Hopkey, Sophy, 164
Hopkinson, Francis, 13
Houston, Sam, 159
Howe, Sir William, 78
Hunt, Sanford B., 67
Hunter, Gen. David F., 22, 171
Huntington, Collis P., 144
Hutchinson, Asa, 124, 126

Isaacs, John D., 52
Ives, James M., 48

Jackson, Andrew, 102, 119
Jefferson, Thomas, 14, 35–37, 43, 80–83, 109, 111
Jones, John Paul, 178

Keene, James R., 152, 154
Kemmler, Willie, 105–108
Kennon, Beverly, 122
Klinefelter, Captain, 91, 93

Langley, Samuel P., 74, 112–116
Lawson, Thomas, 66

Lee, Richard, 13
Lee, Gen. Robt. E., 38, 94–96
L'Enfant, Pierre C., 11
Lewis, Morgan, 111
Lilienthal, Otto, 73
Lincoln, Abraham, 23, 24, 40, 41, 87, 88, 156, 168, 171
Lincoln, Levi, 36
Lincoln, Mary Todd, 136–139
Long, Huey, 156
Longstreet, Gen. James, 86
Louis XIV, King, 78
Low, Frederick, 71
Luttrell, Henry H., 131

MacCrellish, Frederick, 152, 154
McCausland, John, 23
McClellan, George B., 39–41
McCook, Col. Dan, 87
McDonald, Carlos F., 107
McKeon, John, 33
McManigal, Ortie, 148
McNamara, James B., 148
McNamara, John, 146, 148, 150
Madison, James, 12, 13, 36
Manley, Charles M., 114, 115
Mann, William D'Alton, 137
Marbury, William, 36, 37
Marshall, John, 34–37, 83
Marshall, John W., 68, 69
Mason, Charles, 43
Mather, Cotton, 18?
Mather, Increase, 59
Mathias, Charles, 24
Maxcy, Virgil, 122
Monck, Christopher, 180, 181
Morris, Gouverneur, 15
Morse, Wayne, 156
Muybridge, Eadweard J., 152, 153

Nast, Thomas, 173
Norton, Oliver W., 99

Ogle, Charles, 102–104
Otis, Harrison Gray, 147

Palmer, Nathaniel B., 62–64
Paterson, William, 183–186
Penn, Richard, 43
Penn, William, 43
Phips, William, 179–182
Pitt, William, 134
Pullman, George M., 137–140

Randolph, Edmund, 184
Randolph, Jefferson, 82
Randolph, John, 83
Roosevelt, Theodore, 113
Rosencrans, Gen. W.S., 85

Scott, Gen. Winfield, 119, 169
Sequoyah, 118
Seward, William H., 172
Sheridan, William P., 147
Sherman, Roger, 184
Sherman, Gen. William T., 26, 70, 71, 87
Shipley, Jonathan, 133, 134
Sickles, Gen. Dan, 26
Smith, John C., 15
Stanford, Leland, 151-154
Stanley, Edward, 180
Steward, Rev. Nixon B., 87
Stockton, Robert Field, 120, 121
Stowe, Harriet Beecher, 123-129
Strahan, William, 17
Stuart, John, Earl of Bute, 17
Sumner, Charles, 159
Sutter, John A., 68-71
Swartwout, Samuel, 110

Thomas, Gen. George H., 86-87
Thurmond, Strom, 156
Tilden, Samuel J., 26-29, 173, 176
Tutorow, Norman E., 153
Twain, Mark. *See* Clemens, Samuel L., 159

Tweed, William Marcy, 173
Tyler, John, 30-33, 83, 120-122

Upsher, Abel P., 122

Van Buren, Martin, 101-104
Vanderbilt, Cornelius, 46

Waddell, James I., 94-97
Wagenknecht, Edward, 129
Wagner, Webster, 137
Walker, Dr. Mary, 84-88
Wallace, Lew, 22, 23
Waller, William N., 120, 121
Washington, Booker T., 141-144
Washington, Bushrod, 36
Washington, George, 13, 14, 21, 43, 160
Webb, Willard, 39
Webster, Daniel, 31-33, 86
Webster, Fletcher, 32
Wesley, John, 164
Westinghouse, George, 105, 106
Whalley, Edward, 59, 60
Wilkes, John, 132-134
Wilkins, William, 122
Wilson, James, 184
Woodbury, Levi, 102
Woodruff, T.T., 137
Wright, Katherine, 73, 74
Wright, Orville, 72-75, 112
Wright, Wilbur, 73-75, 112